P9-BNV-139

THE BASICS
OF RIFLE
SHOOTING

Produced by the Education and Training Division

A Publication of the National Rifle Association of America

First Edition—May, 1987
© 1987 The National Rifle Association of America

ISBN 0-935998-01-2

13180 7-06

FOREWORD

This handbook offers a basic education in rifle shooting. Written by shooters for people with an interest in learning how to shoot a rifle, it provides the basic knowledge, skills, and attitude necessary to enter and master this exciting sport.

Like any other sport, shooting a rifle is an acquired skill that calls for a step-by-step learning approach. The novice moves from the simple to the complicated, thoroughly learning each step before moving on to the next. This method is not new, but it has one overwhelming advantage —it works!

Beginners often make the mistake of trying to tackle too much too soon, much like a new piano student trying to play Chopin or a first year math student attempting calculus. When you start at the beginning, you learn quickly, building confidence in your ability to perform the skill. Success reinforces success, providing a strong foundation for future rifle shooting activities.

This principle is the same in other sports. For example, in basketball, you begin with the fundamentals -dribbling, passing, shooting. To enhance the initial learning process, you may start with a larger hoop, a closer foul line or a smaller ball. As your skills improve, you move to regulation equipment and game rules, then to one-on-one practice and finally, when you become proficient, into a game with a team. Rifle shooting is no different. To be successful, you learn it step-by-step, building on your skills as you go along. This book will show you how.

Taken individually, each step is simple. Add the right rifle, target, ammunition, and diligence in practice and this book will enable you to hit targets consistently.

There is one other element in learning to shoot a rifle that cannot be found within the pages of this handbook—desire. That's the quality which you have to bring to this endeavor. When you have this book and the desire to learn, you'll find rifle marksmanship is an attainable skill, and you'll be on your way to countless hours of enjoyment.

Good shooting!

ACKNOWLEDGEMENTS

The Basics of Rifle Shooting reflects the concepts and thoughts of instructors, coaches and shooters, who through the years have refined the knowledge and skills used in rifle shooting.

The National Rifle Association gratefully acknowledges the contributions of NRA Certified Rifle Instructors and Training Counselors and others who provided input in the preparation of this handbook.

Jim Carmichel, Shooting Editor, Outdoor Life, and author of numerous articles and books on the shooting sports; member, NRA Board of Directors, and Silhouette Rifle Committee; distinguished firearm and shooting authority.

Robert W. Christina, Ph.D., Professor of Physical Education and Director of the Motor Behavior Research Laboratory, The Pennsylvania State University; shooting sports researcher and author; member, NRA Class B Coach Schools faculty; and member, U.S. Shooting Sports Research Council.

Henry D. Cross, III, Ph.D., Director, Colgate Palmolive Ventures Group; Chairman, U.S. Shooting Sports Research Council; Chairman, International Shooter Development Fund; member, All American Rifle Team, Georgetown University; Distinguished Highpower Rifleman.

H. T. "Tom " Davison, Texas State 4-H Program Leader; Chairman, National 4-H Shooting Sports Development Committee; member, NRA Board of Directors, Education and Training and Junior & Collegiate Programs Committees; 1985 National NRA Public Service Award Recipient.

Phillip B. Dean, Principal, Baker Intermediate School, Damascus, Maryland; member, NRA Education and Training Committee and Special Task Force on Schools; contributing author to many NPA training publications; developer and teacher of firearm and shooting programs in schools.

Reinhart Fajen, founder and President of Reinhart Fajen, Incorporated; maker of gunstocks for rifles and shotguns since 1939.

Robert H. Johnston, Ph.D., Dean, College of Fine and Applied Arts, Rochester Institute of Technology, New York; member, NRA Education and Training Committee; Director, NPA/RIT Gunsmithing Schools Program; distinguished scholar and published author.

Grace and Roy Knight, Proprietors, Knights Custom Gun Shop; he has been a firearm retailer and custom rifle maker since 1944 and is a published author and former high school industrial arts teacher.

Steven K. Moore, Director of Support Services, North Florida Council, Boy Scouts of America; Director, Shooting Sports, BSA National Camp Schools; Director, Field Sports, National Boy Scout Jamboree; Director, NRA National Junior Smallbore Rifle Camp; staff member, NRA Training Counselor Workshops.

Ferris Pindell, President, Pindell's Precision Tooling; research and development engineer; winner of 11 Bench Rest Rifle World Records and 10 National Championships; member, Bench Rest Hall of Fame.

Sue Ann Sandusky, Assistant Professor, Department of Social Sciences, West Point Military Academy; World Rifle Champion; member, NRA Education and Training and International Competitions Committees; Athlete Delegate and Alternate to the House of Delegates, United States Olympic Committee.

Marlin R. Scarborough, former member, NRA Board of Directors; former member, South Dakota Board of Regents of Higher Education and South Dakota Game, Fish and Parks Commission; Distinguished Highpower Rifleman.

Jack V. Slack, Vice President of Marketing, Leupold & Stevens, Incorporated; in the scope manufacturing business since 1959; a master highpower rifle competitor and avid hunter.

Alan W. Sexton, Ph.D., Professor Emeritus, Department of Physical Medicine and Rehabilitation, University of Colorado School of Medicine; member, NRA Board of Directors; Chairman, NRA Education and Training and Vice Chairman, Grants-In-Aid Committees; Distinguished Rifleman; past captain, National Civilian Rifle Team.

Joseph S. Smith, Lt. Col., Retired, U.S. Army; Retired Deputy Director of Civilian Marksmanship, Department of the Army; distinguished national leader in junior and rifle marksmanship programs.

Ken N. Waite, Jr., Regional Manager, Remington Arms Company.

Lones Wigger, Jr., Lt. Col., Retired, U.S. Army; Director, NRA U.S. Shooting Team Division; former officer in charge, International Rifle Branch, U.S. Army Marksmanship Training Unit; competitive shooter for 36 years, he has won more than 70 national individual championships, been a member of 20 U.S. International Shooting Teams which included four Olympic teams where he won 2 gold medals. He has won 107 medals and established 29 World Records in these competitions.

C O N T E N T S

INTRODUCTION

Every year thousands of Americans take up the challenging sport of rifle shooting. Some become involved and compete in prestigious tournaments, win awards and even set records. Others want to pursue the sport of hunting. But for most people, the objective is much more basic. They get into rifle shooting simply for the fun of it.

Regardless of your reason, riflery is rewarding if you learn the basics. The modern rifle is sophisticated, precise and—in skilled hands—capable of providing many enjoyable times. The essence of rifle shooting is marksmanship, the ability to hit the target you have selected with one shot. If you're going to get the most out of your rifle—the most fun, the most proficiency—first learn safe and skillful shooting. That is what this book is all about.

An objective of The Basics of Rifle Shooting is to answer some of your questions: How does the rifle work? What kind of rifle is best for me? How can I be sure I'm using it properly and safely? What's the best way to find others to share and enhance my enjoyment of the sport? In the following pages, we'll take a close look at all these questions. We'll explain the basics, show you how to choose your rifle, and introduce you to the fundamentals of shooting. This book can be your passport to a lifetime of safe and rewarding participation in this challenging sport.

PART ONE

KNOWING
YOUR
RIFLE

CHAPTER 1

RIFLE PARTS AND HOW THEY WORK

To the casual observer, most rifles may look alike. However, rifles come in many variations and are surprisingly versatile pieces of equipment. They also come with a vocabulary all their own. Learning that vocabulary is essential to understanding how a rifle works.

The rifle is divided into three major parts, each representing one of its three major assembly groups. They are:

- **The Stock**: the handle by which the rifle is held;
- **The Barrel**: the metal tube through which the projectile (bullet) passes when the rifle is fired;
- **The Action**: the section of the rifle containing the moving parts that load, fire and unload the rifle.

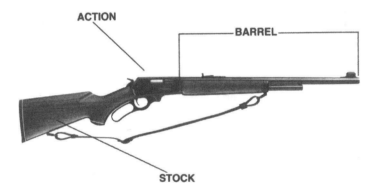

MAJOR RIFLE PARTS

Let's look at each of these major parts.

THE STOCK

Besides being perhaps the most visually pleasing part of a firearm, the stock has special design features that afford the shooter comfort, ease of handling and maximum shooting accuracy. Most stocks are made of wood, but many modern stocks are now made of fiberglass or other synthetic materials. The stock is divided into four parts:

3

RIFLE PARTS

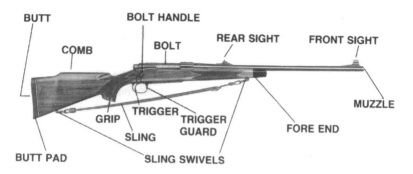

The *butt* is the rear portion of the stock. It is generally contoured or slightly curved to fit comfortably against the shoulder.

The *comb* is the top portion of the stock, upon which the shooter rests his cheek.

The *grip*, sometimes called the pistol grip or "small of the stock," is the area where the hand grasps the stock when squeezing the trigger.

The *fore end* is the part of the stock that extends underneath the barrel. This is the area where the other hand holds the rifle to support it. In some rifles, the fore end is separate from the rest of the stock and often referred to as the forearm.

THE BARREL

There is more to this simple looking tube than meets the eye. The barrel has several different parts, and each has specific jobs that work together to cause the projectile to pass accurately to the target.

The hollow inside of the barrel—the hole through which the bullet passes—is called the *bore*. The bore is measured in hundredths of an inch or in millimeters. This measurement is called the *caliber* of the rifle. The wider the diameter of the bore, the larger the caliber and, therefore, the larger the size of the bullet it will accommodate.

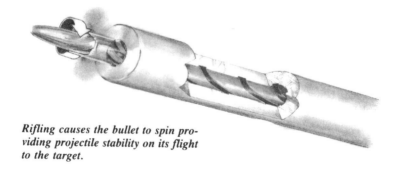

Rifling causes the bullet to spin providing projectile stability on its flight to the target.

The opening through which the bullet leaves the barrel is called the *muzzle*. The rear of the barrel is called the *breech*.

The *chamber* is located at the breech end of the barrel. That is the portion of the bore into which one round of ammunition (cartridge) is placed for firing. Chambers are shaped identically to the ammunition. As long as you are using the proper size ammunition, the fit should be perfect.

For its remaining length, the bore of the barrel is lined with a series of spiral *grooves*. The flat, raised ridges of metal standing between the grooves are called *lands*. When a bullet passes through the barrel, the lands cut into the bullet and cause it to spin. This spinning action makes the bullet more stable and accurate in its flight towards the target just as spinning makes a toy top or gyroscope stable. Together the lands and grooves inside the barrel are known as *rifling*, which is how the rifle got its name.

THE ACTION

The action allows the shooter to load, shoot and unload the rifle. Several different designs or types of actions have been developed to accomplish the action's purpose.

Loading is achieved by first opening the action. This allows you to place a cartridge in the chamber. With the cartridge in place, the *bolt* or *breech block* is then closed. In most rifles, opening and closing the action cocks the firing pin thus readying the rifle for firing. However, some rifles must be cocked separately.

Firing takes place when you squeeze the *trigger*. This allows the *firing pin* to be driven forward.

When you open the action after firing, the used cartridge case is usually ejected so that a new one can be loaded and fired.

In addition, many rifle actions have two other features which add to the convenience and safe handling of the rifle—the magazine and safety.

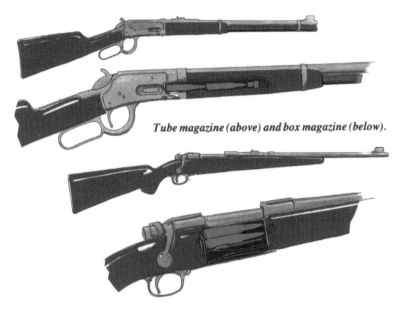

Tube magazine (above) and box magazine (below).

The **magazine** is a container attached to the rifle into which several cartridges can be placed. Most rifles can be loaded manually using one cartridge at a time. Many, however, use a magazine to expedite loading. Although no rifle chamber can accommodate more than one cartridge at a time, the magazine makes it possible for you to load a new cartridge into the chamber without having to load it by hand. When the action is opened and closed, a new cartridge is automatically pushed from the magazine into the chamber. The rifle can be fired repeatedly until the magazine is empty.

The two most common magazine types are a "box type" located inside the bottom portion of the action, and a "tube type" located under the barrel or in the stock.

The **safety** is a mechanical device. When activated or placed in the "on" position, it is designed to block the operation of the trigger or firing pin, thus preventing the rifle from firing. To fire, the safety is placed in the "off" position. Remember, the safety is mechanical and therefore, subject to malfunction. It must *never* be depended on as a replacement for following the safety rules.

6

The safety on the above rifle is shown by an arrow. The location of the safety can vary depending on the model of the rifle.

Nothing takes the place of always pointing the muzzle in a safe direction. At best a safety is only extra insurance. Due to the false sense of security safeties can create—"I thought the safety was on," they may have actually contributed to more mishaps than they have prevented. Get the point—YOU are the safety!

TYPES OF ACTIONS

There are six popular types of cartridge rifle actions. To give a general idea of how these actions operate, the following list describes the loading and unloading procedures for some of the more common rifle designs. It should be noted that there are many operational variations for these as well as other types of action designs. *You must thoroughly study and understand your rifle's operation manual before using your rifle.*

BOLT

The bolt action rifle operates on a lift, pull and push sequence similar to a door bolt. The bolt action is probably the most common type of action. Many feel it is the strongest, most accurate of the action types.

To Load Box Magazine (nonremovable clip)

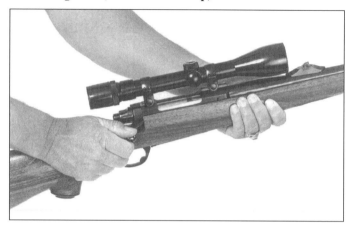

1. Open action by lifting bolt handle up and to the rear.

2. Lay cartridge in open action and press downward into magazine. Repeat process to load additional cartridges.

3. Push bolt handle forward and down, pushing cartridge into chamber and locking action.

To Unload

1. Open action, ejecting cartridge from chamber.
2a. Actions with releasable floor plates:

- Release floor plate to open magazine.

- Allow cartridges to fall free of magazine.

- Return floor plate to locked position.

2b. Actions with nonremovable floor plates:

- Continue to open and close action, working each cartridge through it until the rifle is empty.

3. Visually check chamber and magazine to be sure gun is completely unloaded.

To Load Box Magazine (removable)

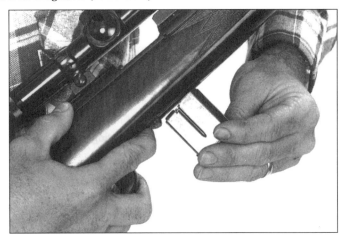

1. Open action and press magazine release.
2. Remove magazine from rifle.

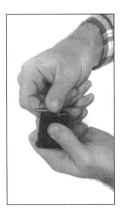

3.   Load magazine with cartridges.

4. Return loaded magazine to rifle.

5. Close bolt, loading cartridge into chamber.

To Unload
1. Open action ejecting cartridge from chamber.
2. Remove magazine from rifle.
3. Remove cartridges from magazine.
4. Visually check to be sure rifle is unloaded,

PUMP

On pump or slide action rifles, the forearm of the stock is pumped back and forth to open and close the action. Experienced marksmen, using a pump action rifle, can quickly load, fire, and eject the spent cartridge while keeping the rifle pointed towards the target.

To Load Tube Magazine

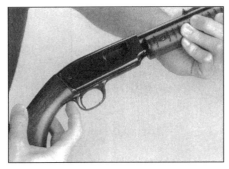

1. Open action by pressing action release and pulling forearm to rear.

2. To open magazine, pull plunger past magazine cartridge opening.

3. Place cartridges in magazine opening, letting them slide down the magazine tube.
4. Return plunger tube to original position and lock in place; push forearm forward to close action.

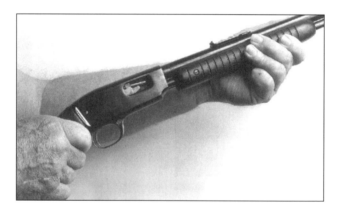

5. To feed cartridge from magazine to chamber, open and close action.

To Unload
1. Depress action release.
2. Open and close the action until there are no cartridges being ejected from the rifle. Count the number of cartridges or empty cases to be sure they equal the number loaded.
3. With action open, visually check chamber and magazine to be sure rifle is completely unloaded.

LEVER

The action on a lever action rifle is opened by pulling the cocking lever downward and forward away from the stock. It is closed by simply returning the lever back to its original position. Lever action rifles, like pump action rifles, also allow the rapid reloading of additional cartridges.

To Load

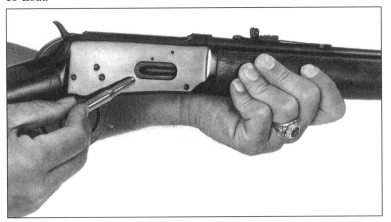

1. Load cartridges into magazine through loading port on the side of the action.

2. Open and close the action, feeding a cartridge from the magazine into the chamber.

To Unload

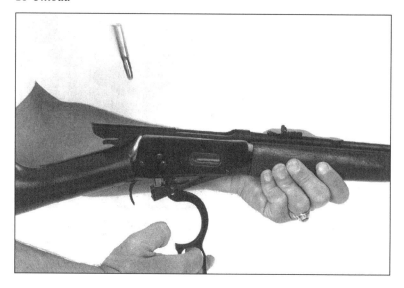

I . Open and close the action by lowering and raising the lever until there are no cartridges being ejected from the rifle. Count the number of cartridges or empty cases to be sure they equal the same number loaded.
2. With the action open, visually check the chamber and magazine to be sure the gun is completely unloaded.

SEMI- AUTOMATIC

These actions are sometimes appropriately called repeaters or auto-loaders. Each time a semi-automatic rifle is fired the cartridge provides the energy to operate the action.

To Load

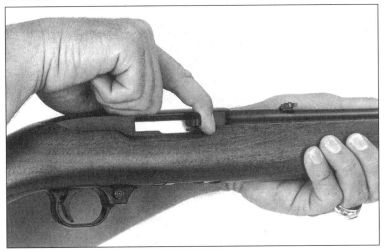

1. Pull bolt open and lock.

2. Remove magazine and load.

3. Return loaded magazine to rifle.
4. Close action to load cartridge in chamber.

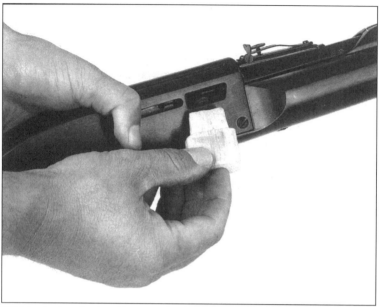

Some semi-automatics do not have a system for locking the action open. In this situation, a wood block should be placed in the action to show that the rifle is unloaded and clear.

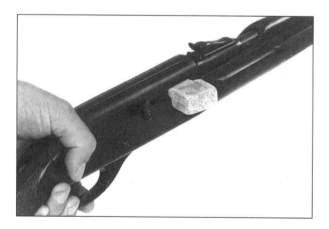

To Unload

1. Open action, ejecting cartridge from chamber, and lock action open.
2. Remove magazine and remove all cartridges from it.

3. With action open, visually check chamber and magazine to be sure rifle is unloaded.

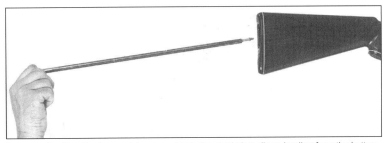

Some semi-automatics have a tube magazine in the stock that allows loading from the butt or side.

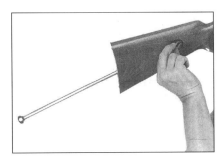

HINGE

The hinge action opens similar to the movement of a door hinge. When the release lever is pushed to one side, the barrel(s) swing downward away from the breech block. Hinge action rifles may have one, two or three barrels. Double rifles are built either as an "over and under" or a "side by side," depending on the placement of the barrels. Three-barreled guns usually have a combination of shotgun and rifle barrels and are often called *drillings*.

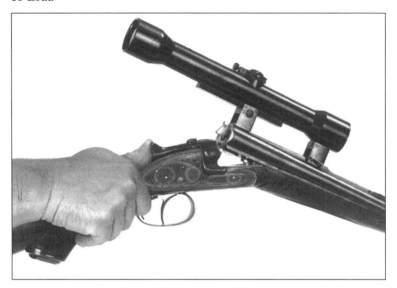

1. Open action by pushing action release lever to side and tipping barrels downward.

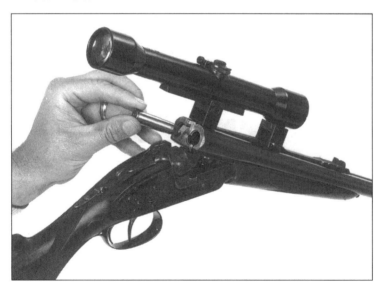

2. Place cartridge(s) into chamber(s).
3. Return barrels to original closed position.

To Unload
1. Open action in same manner as when loading.
2. Remove cartridges.

FALLING BLOCK

The falling block action utilizes a breech block instead of a bolt. The action is opened by lowering the trigger guard or the small lever under it that causes the breech block to "fall" down and away from the barrel. Raising the lever closes the action and covers the breech end of the barrel. Falling block rifles are all single shot rifles.

To Load

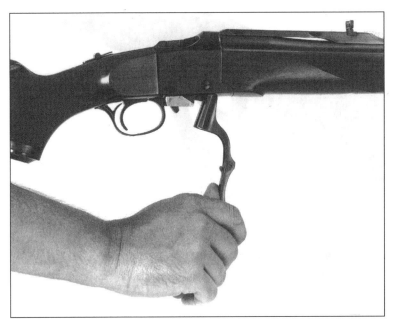

1. Open action by lowering lever.

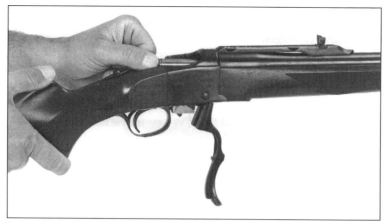

2. Load cartridge into chamber.

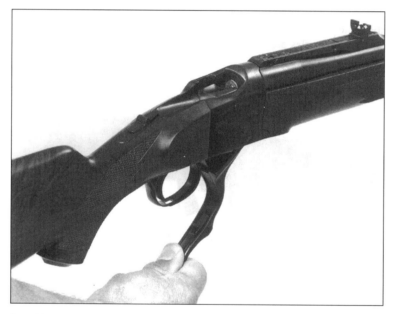

3. Close action by pulling lever up to original position. (Caution: Some falling block rifles cock on opening, others do not.)

To Unload
1. Open action.
2. Remove cartridge.

SIGHTS

Sights enable you to aim the rifle. Although there are many different types of sights, they generally fall into three categories: *optical sights, open sights, and aperture sights.*

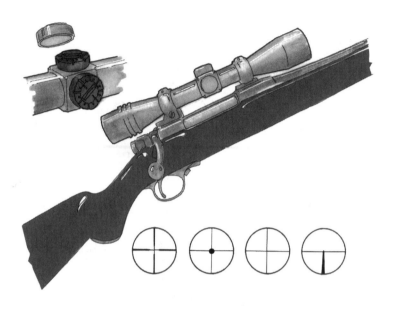

Pictured above are some of the more common reticles used in optical sights. Left to right: duplex, dot, crosshair, and post. Choice is largely a matter of personal preference. The reticle can be easily adjusted by turning the adjustment knobs on the scope in the direction you wish to move your shots on the target.

Optical Sights are small telescopes, mounted atop the barrel or action. They are a good sight for new shooters because they are simple to use. Optical sights have a *reticle* (crosshairs or dot) that acts as an aiming point and is aligned with the target. Optical sights give the shooter an advantage because they make it possible to see both the sight and the target in clear focus. Optical sights also magnify the target and make it possible to aim more precisely. Two types of scopes are available— "fixed" magnification and those with "variable" (adjustable) magnification. *Scope mounts* are used to attach optical sights to rifles. It's important that they be of the right design and size for the rifle and scope. Mount screws must be tight to ensure consistent accuracy.

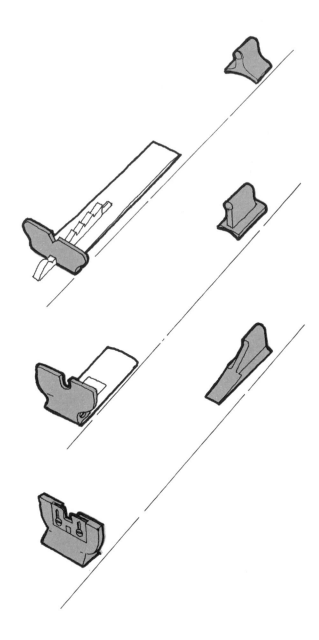

Open sights are available in a variety of adjustable and fixed designs.

Open Sights are standard equipment on most factory rifles. They include an open rear sight (a notch or "V" located near the breech end of the barrel) and a front sight (a post or bead) located near the muzzle. To aim, the shooter aligns the front and rear sights and aims the aligned sights at the target.

Aperture Sights are usually mounted on the rear part of the rifle action and are often called "peep" sights because they have a small hole in the rear sight that you look through in aiming. When using this type of sight, simply align the front sight in the center of the rear sight opening. When the eye looks through a small opening, it is naturally drawn to the center of the opening where the light is brightest. These sights make aligning the sights much easier and more precise than with open sights, but they are not as fast or easy to use when shots must be fired very quickly.

Aperture rear sights, scopes and some open sights can be precisely adjusted without special tools. Sight adjustment is absolutely essential because it enables you to get your shots to hit the target exactly where your sights are aimed. Generally, you can make both "elevation" (up or down) and "windage" (right or left) adjustments. The standard rule when adjusting rear sights is to move them in the same direction you want to *move the location of the shot on the target*. With scopes it is necessary to move the reticle in the *opposite* direction you want to move the shots.

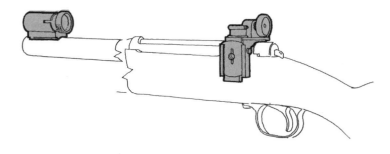

Aperture sights are popular with target shooters because they are easily adjusted.

SCOPE USAGE

A General Guideline

Magnification	Uses
1 to 2.5 X	Moving targets, quick reaction shots, big game hunting
3 to 6 X	General hunting and recreational shooting
6 to 10 X	Varmint, silhouette, informal target shooting
12 to 36 X	Bench rest, smallbore prone, silhouette, other specialized target shooting events

1. Safety rules for using a scope are:
   a. Scopes mounted on rifles are used only for aiming at identified targets you intend to shoot. Never use a rifle scope for observing distant objects or searching for game.
   b. Always keep a safe distance between the eye and the back of the scope when firing highpower rifles with considerable recoil.

2. Higher magnification also magnifies any movement of the rifle, therefore, making it appear more difficult to hold the rifle steady.

3. The higher the magnification the closer the target appears, but the smaller the field of vision.

4. A variable scope can be used to allow a choice of scope power.

PART I

1. What are the three major parts of a rifle?

2. The lands and grooves in the bore of a rifle are called
   _____.

3. The two most common magazine types are _____ and
   _____.

4. Name the six popular types of rifle actions.

5. The three categories of rifle sights are:

6. The measurement of the bore in 1/100 of inches or millimeters is called the
   _____ of the rifle.

7. The opening through which the projectile leaves the barrel is called the
   _____.

8. That portion of the barrel into which a round of ammunition is placed for
   shooting is called the _____.

CHAPTER 2

To fire a rifle, ammunition must be inserted into the chamber at the breech end of the barrel. The types of ammunition available today are as diverse as the rifle itself. A number of different sizes and shapes have been developed to fit every sporting need. All modern rifle ammunition, however, is made up of four basic parts-the case, primer, powder and bullet. Together they form a rifle *cartridge*.

CARTRIDGE PARTS AND FUNCTION

Rifles requiring a cartridge depend on the burning of gunpowder within the case to produce the extremely high gas pressure that propels the bullet through the barrel and to the target.

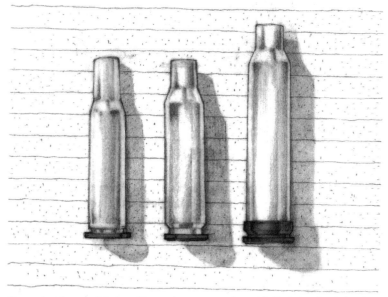

Cases come in several designs. The most common are rimmed (left), rimless (center) and belted (right).

- The **case** is the container into which the other ammunition parts are assembled. A metal, typically brass, is used in its construction. Cases come in many types and shapes. There are two basic types: rimfire and centerfire. The difference between the two is the location of the primer.

RIMFIRE

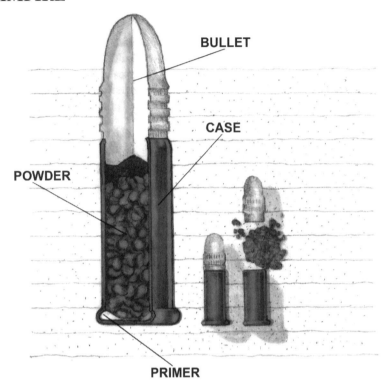

BULLET

CASE

POWDER

PRIMER

● The **primer** is an impact-sensitive chemical compound that ignites when hit by the firing pin and in turn ignites the powder charge. In *rimfire* ammunition, the priming chemical is contained inside the hollow rim at the base of the cartridge case. The rim is soft enough that when the firing pin strikes it a small dent is created. This indentation crushes and ignites the priming compound, causing it to ignite the powder charge. In *centerfire* ammunition, the primer is a separate component located in the center of the cartridge case base. The firing pin strikes the primer and the resulting indentation sets off the ignition process.

The actual mechanics of firing are the same whether the ammunition used is rimfire or centerfire.

CENTERFIRE

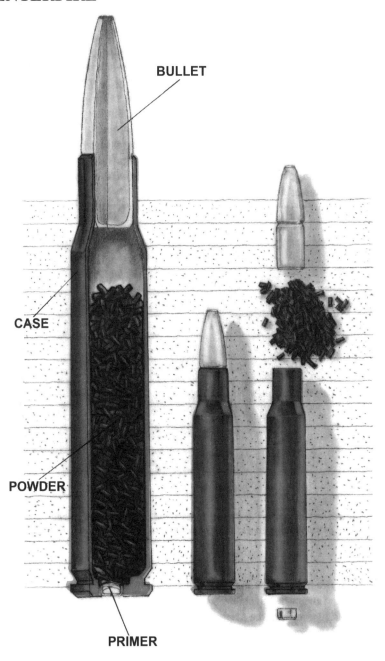

BULLET

CASE

POWDER

PRIMER

- The **powder charge** is a chemical compound that is designed to burn rapidly and produce a high volume of gas. Modern *smokeless gunpowder* is a combustible solid, not an explosive. When ignited by the primer flame, the expanding powder gas provides the force to propel the bullet through the bore and out the muzzle.
- The **bullet** is the projectile that is shot from the rifle to the target. It is manufactured of lead and may also have a *jacket* of a harder metal such as copper. Like the rifle bore, bullets are measured in calibers. Their shape, weight and construction vary with the caliber of the rifle used and the shooter's purpose. The size or caliber of the bullet must be identical with the caliber of the bore or an extremely unsafe condition can result. Some bullets have soft or hollow points which allow the bullet to flatten and expand in diameter when it hits the target.

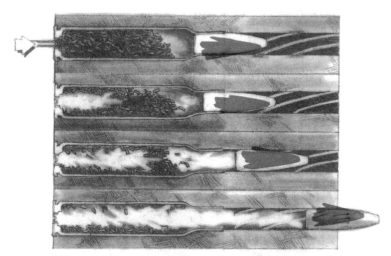

1) Firing pin strikes primer; 2) Primer ignites and in turn ignites powder; 3) Burning powder forms gases; 4) Expanding gases propel bullet.

Rifles **fire** by means of a chain reaction that begins when the trigger is moved and ends when the bullet's flight ceases. The first step occurs when the trigger releases the firing pin and it strikes the primer, causing the priming compound to ignite. The flame generated by the primer ignites the powder charge. The rapidly burning powder produces a high volume of gas under very high pressure. Gas under pressure seeks the path of least resistance. Since the breech end of the barrel is blocked and the muzzle end is open, the gas takes the path through the bore and out the muzzle. Standing in the way of the expanding gas, however, is the bullet. But since it gives the least resistance, the gas pushes it along as it travels to the muzzle. All this is done in a split second to cause the bullet to travel at velocities (the speed of the bullet measured in feet per second) that commonly vary from 1,000 to 4,000 feet per second. The force of air resistance causes this velocity to diminish as the bullet travels toward the target. The force of gravity causes the bullet to gradually fall to the earth.

RELOADING RIFLE AMMUNITION

If you do much rifle shooting, you may be interested in reloading your own rifle ammunition. Centerfire ammunition can be reloaded because the spent primer can be removed and replaced. Rimfire ammunition cannot be reloaded because the primer cannot be readily replaced. Many shooters reload ammunition because it saves money, offers greater versatility in the types of ammunition loads available, and improves accuracy. Reloading is an enjoyable and interesting hobby. A wide selection of reloading equipment and components are available. Reloaders must, in every instance, carefully follow all current manufacturers' recommendations for the various equipment, components and loads that are used. The NRA Metallic Cartridge Reloading Course is available to those interested in reloading.

There are many excellent reloading manuals available. Be sure to follow recommended loading data.

RIMFIRE CARTRIDGES

.22 Short

.22 Long Rifle

CENTERFIRE CARTRIDGES

.22 Hornet

.222 Remington

.223 Remington

.22-250 Remington

.243 Winchester

.264 Winchester Magnum

.270 Winchester

7mm Remington Magnum

.30-30 Winchester

.308 Winchester

,30-'06

.338 Winchester Magnum

.375 Holland & Holland Magnum

.45-70 Government

.458 Winchester Magnum

Each rifle caliber has a wide selection of cartridges in that caliber from which to choose. Performance capabilities vary considerably according to their design and intended use, particularly in regard to hunting. Although not all calibers are addressed, the following chart gives you general information from which to pursue further study. Ammunition catalogs and reloading manuals are good sources for indepth study.

Rimfire Caliber:

.22 - the most common cartridge, used for informal recreational and competitive target shooting and small game hunting.

Centerfire Calibers:

.17 -.22 (5.6mm) - Used for informal recreational and competitive target shooting and small game and varmint hunting. Popular cartridges include. 222 Remington, .22-250 Remington and .223. Inexpensive .223 military cases for reloading are commonly available.

.243 (6mm) - .250 - Used for hunting deer, antelope and similar size game and also for benchrest competition and varmint hunting. Popular cartridges include . 243 Winchester and .25-06 Remington.

.264 (6.5mm) - .284 (7mm) - Adequate for hunting most North American big game. The .270 Winchester and 7mm Remington Magnum are quite popular.

.30 (7.62mm) - Considered by many to be the all-around and most versatile caliber. Used for hunting most big game and for informal recreational and competitive target shooting. The. 30-06 is by far the most common with the .308 Winchester (7.62mm NATO service cartridge) and .300 Winchester Magnum also being popular.

.323 (8mm) - .358 - Used primarily for hunting the largest species of North American game. A popular cartridge is the .338 Winchester Magnum.

.375 -.458 - Used primarily for hunting the largest species of African game. The. 375 Holland & Holland Magnum and.458 Winchester Magnum are the most common.

1. In many cases the designations used by industry for cartridges are only nominal caliber designations. Over the years this has been necessary in order to differentiate between different cartridges using the same caliber of bullet—i.e. 6x47, 6mm PPC, .243 Winchester, .244 Remington, 6mmX.284, 6mm Remington International, .240 Weatherby Magnum cartridges all use .243 caliber bullets.

2. Cartridges are generally identified by caliber and the name of the developer or initial manufacturer—i.e. .257 Roberts or .243 Winchester.

3. When a cartridge designation includes two numbers, the first number indicates the bullet caliber. The second number has a wide variety of meanings. For instance, .30 –06 indicates that this is .30 caliber cartridge was introduced in 1906; .45-70 means that the cartridge was originally designated for 70 grains of black powder—the term has stuck even though modern cartridges use smokeless powder; .250-3000 means that the bullet is supposed to travel at a velocity of 3,000 feet per second. The key point to remember is that the two numbers specifically identify the type of cartridge.

PART I

1. Rifle cartridges are made up of what four parts?

2. The two basic types of rifle cartridges are _____ and
_____.

3. Briefly describe the firing sequence of a rifle cartridge.

4. What are some reasons for reloading ammunition?

CHAPTER 3

When you participate in shooting sports, you're also assuming a vital *responsibility* that affects other lives. It is vitally important to learn and practice all of the rifle safety rules.

When handled correctly and used properly, a rifle is not dangerous. Rifles, like any other precision machine, instrument or piece of sports equipment, are manufactured to perform a specific task and can do so at no risk to the user or others. If a rifle is handled incorrectly or recklessly, without regard for the safety rules, then accidents can occur.

Rifle safety is a simple but ongoing process. You must first acquire a **knowledge** of how to handle rifles safely, then develop and maintain proper safe handling **skills** through practice. But the most important element to being safe is **attitude**. Safety knowledge and skills are of little value unless you have the attitude to use them all of the time. Being safe means that you are consciously keeping your gun under control. Always be alert to, and conscious of, your rifle's capabilities, and be aware of what might happen if it is used improperly.

There are basic gun safety rules that must always be applied. They fall into two major categories: those you must follow when *handling* a rifle and those you must follow when *shooting* one.

RULES FOR SAFE RIFLE HANDLING

Three basic rules apply whenever you are handling a rifle—under any circumstances. Rule No. 1 is the "Golden Rule of Gun Safety."

1. **<u>ALWAYS</u> keep the gun pointed in a safe direction.** A *safe direction* means that the gun is pointed so that even if it were to go off it would not cause injury or damage. The key to this rule is to control where the muzzle or front end of the barrel is pointed at all times. Common sense dictates the safest direction, depending on different circumstances.

2. **<u>ALWAYS</u> keep your finger off of the trigger until ready to shoot.** When holding a gun, rest your trigger finger outside the trigger guard alongside the gun. Until you are actually ready to fire, do not touch the trigger.

3. __ALWAYS__ **keep the gun unloaded until ready to use.** Whenever you pick up a gun, always keep the gun pointed in a safe direction, keep your finger off the trigger, engage the mechanical safety if possible, and remove the ammunition source (magazine and ammunition from chamber).

RULES FOR SAFE RIFLE USE AND STORAGE

When you're actually engaged in shooting—whether in hunting, recreational practice or competition—these basic rules must always be followed.

1. **Know your target and what is beyond.** Be absolutely sure you have identified your target beyond any doubt. Equally important, be aware of the area beyond your target. This means observing your prospective area of fire before you shoot. Never fire in a direction in which there are people or any other potential for mishap. Think first. Shoot second.

2. **Know how to safely use the gun.** Before handling a gun, learn how it operates. Know its basic parts, how to open and close the action safely and how to remove safely any ammunition from the gun or magazine. Remember, a gun's mechanical safety device is never foolproof. Nothing can ever replace safe gun handling.

3. **Be sure the gun is safe to operate.** Just like other tools, guns need regular maintenance to remain operable. Regular cleaning and proper storage are a part of the gun's general upkeep. If there is any question concerning a gun's ability to function, a competent gunsmith should look at it.

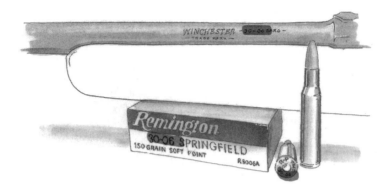

4. **Use only the correct ammunition for your gun.** Only BBs, pellets, cartridges, or shells designed for a particular gun can be fired safely in that gun. Most guns have the ammunition type stamped on the barrel. Ammunition can be identified by information printed on the box and sometimes stamped on the cartridge. Do not shoot the gun unless you know you have the proper ammunition.

5. **Wear eye and ear protection as appropriate.** Guns are loud and the noise can cause hearing damage. They can also emit debris and hot gas that could cause eye injury. For these reasons, safety glasses and ear protection are recommended.

6. **Never use alcohol or drugs before or while shooting.** Alcohol, as well as any other substance likely to impair normal mental or physical bodily functions must not be used before or while handling or shooting guns.

7. **Store guns so they are not accessible to unauthorized persons.** Several factors should be considered when you decide on where and how you intend to store your guns. Your particular needs will be a major part of the consideration. Safe and secure storage requires that untrained individuals (especially children) be denied access to your gun.

Be aware that certain types of guns and many shooting activities require additional safety precautions.

SHOOTING RANGES

The first thing to do when arriving at a range is to learn the range rules.

    The supervised shooting range is one of the safest places to enjoy shooting. The operators of most ranges use standard range commands to control the shooting and to promote uniform safe practices. The purpose of range commands and rules is to let everyone shoot safely. In every case, the undisputed boss is the Range Officer. That person is the one giving the commands and monitoring all shooters to be sure they are complying with the safety rules. As a shooter, it's your responsibility to obey and respect him. Below are two of the standard range commands you may hear a **Range Officer** use:

1. "Commence Firing"
2. "Cease Firing"

No matter how formal or informal the shooting circumstances, these two commands are absolute. "Commence firing" means you may begin shooting when you are ready. "Cease firing" means stop shooting *immediately*. In fact, it means more than that. Cease firing means that if you are in the process of squeezing the trigger, you immediately stop, open the action, unload the rifle and lay it down and keep your hands off it. If for some reason the rifle's action cannot be opened readily, then stop shooting, place the mechanical safety on, and lay your rifle down. Immediately let the Range Officer know that your gun is loaded. When you hear the "cease firing" command, absolutely do not fire the shot.

Depending upon the shooting facility, the number of people shooting, the type of shooting equipment being used or other variables, additional commands may be used. Generally these additional commands direct the flow of shooters to and from the firing line, provide necessary instructions, or inform the shooters of time remaining.

Regardless of the shooting conditions, you have an important responsibility. If you see an unsafe situation in which someone could get hurt, then it is your responsibility to call "Cease Fire." Don't wait for the Range Officer. Remember, always use common sense.

PART I

1. In order to be safe with a rifle, what three elements must be in place?

2. What is the golden rule of gun safety?

3. List the three rules for safe rifle handling.

4. Briefly describe how you can determine whether your rifle and ammunition are compatible.

5. Why is it so important to be sure what is beyond your target?

6. Knowledge and skills are of little value in being safe unless you have the _____ to use them all the time.

7. List two of the standard range commands used by a range officer.

CHAPTER 4

Your rifle is a piece of precision equipment. Like any item of value, it must receive proper care if it is to operate correctly and safely. Unlike many other items of sports equipment, however, your rifle is built to last a lifetime. And it will—if you exercise diligence in caring for it.

CLEANING

Ideally, you should make a habit of cleaning your rifle each time it is used. A rifle that is cleaned regularly will shoot more accurately and reliably. Cleaning also preserves the finish and value of the rifle. Cleaning is *essential* when the rifle has been stored for an extended period or has been exposed to dirt or moisture. Don't use a dirty gun; make sure it's cleaned thoroughly before use.

Prior to cleaning the rifle, be sure the action is open and the rifle is *unloaded*. For absolute safety, the action should always be kept open during cleaning and ammunition should *not* be present.

Six basic materials are needed to clean a rifle:
1. Cleaning rod with bore brush and attachment to hold patches (must be proper size for bore of rifle)
2. Cloth patches
3. Bore cleaning solvent
4. Light gun oil
5. Clean cloth
6. Small brush

THE BASIC STEPS IN CLEANING

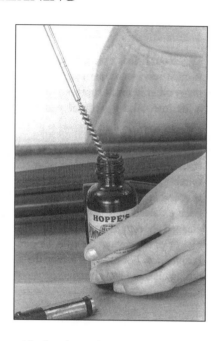

1. Place bore brush on cleaning rod, wet with cleaning solvent and work it back and forth in the bore to loosen residue and fouling.

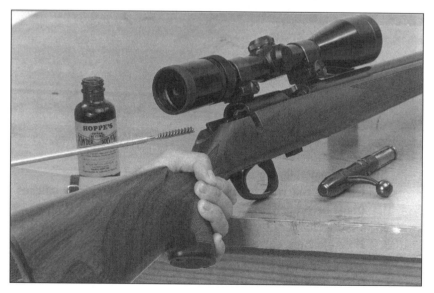

2. To remove the loosened residue and fouling from the bore, run a series of patches through it until they appear clean. Finally, push an oiled patch through the bore. Repeat steps one and two if the patches do not come out clean.

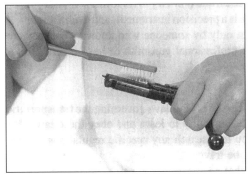

3. Clean any remaining foreign materials from the rifle and particularly the rifle action with a small brush or cloth.

4. Wipe all exposed metal surfaces with a silicone or lightly oiled cloth.

To avoid causing rust after the rifle is cleaned, don't touch the metal. Instead, handle the gun by the stock.

Don't neglect your ammunition either. Sand or dirt collected on the ammunition can damage the chamber or the bore of your rifle. Check it for foreign material before using.

REPAIRS

Beginning shooters should leave repairs to experts. If your rifle is not functioning properly, don't use it and don't try to fix it yourself until you are qualified to do so. A rifle is a precision instrument, and even a minor repair should be undertaken only by someone who knows what they are doing. Take your rifle to a professional gunsmith or have it sent back to the manufacturer for repair.

TRANSPORTATION

Many states and municipalities have laws governing the transportation of firearms. You have a responsibility to learn and obey these laws. It is especially important for you to research any specific regulations in states or cities to which you will be traveling.

Federal law provides that notwithstanding any state or local law, a person is entitled to transport a firearm from any place where he may lawfully possess and carry such firearm to any other place where he may lawfully possess and carry such firearm if, during the transportation, the firearm is unloaded and the firearm and ammunition are in the trunk of the vehicle. In a case of a vehicle

Rifles should be cased and properly stored for transporting.

without a compartment separate from the driver's compartment, the firearm or ammunition shall be contained in a locked container other than the glove compartment or console.

Guns should be packed and stored where they will be safe and will not attract the attention of someone who might steal them. Some jurisdictions may require that they be separate from the ammunition.

STORING FIREARMS

Before you decide how and where you are going to keep your rifle and ammunition, consider safety, storage conditions, access by others and your personal needs. Many people are naturally intrigued by guns and the temptation to pick one up is very real for adults and children alike. That could spell trouble if the person is too young or inexperienced to handle the firearm safely. Security is another factor. Unfortunately, guns are often desirable booty for thieves.

For all these reasons, it is wise to find a secure and convenient location for your shooting equipment. Many manufacturers offer fine wooden cabinets to display and secure your guns. Some gun owners prefer to have their guns in locked metal vaults or storage places where they are out of sight and out of reach. If you choose storage that requires a lock, be sure you keep your keys in a place where casual visitors and youngsters are not likely to find them.

Always store your rifle unloaded. When removing a firearm for handling and cleaning, always remember to follow the safety rules and double check to be sure the chamber is empty.

Ammunition should be kept in a cool, dry place. Many rifle owners prefer to store their guns and ammunition separately to minimize the chances of an accident.

A lockable storage cabinet provides a secure and attractive way to enjoy your rifles.

PART I

1. Describe why it is important to keep your rifle clean.

2. List the basic materials needed to clean a cartridge rifle.

3. What are the two primary things that must be done before you begin to clean a rifle?

4. Outline the basic procedures used in cleaning a cartridge rifle.

5. Describe how you would store your rifle and ammunition safely in your home.

6. When storing, to prevent rust it is best to handle a rifle by the

_____.

PART TWO

BASIC
SHOOTING
SKILLS

CHAPTER I

THE FUNDAMENTALS OF RIFLE SHOOTING

Now that you know how your rifle works, how to handle it safely and how to care for it, you're ready to learn how to shoot it. As you'll soon see, there's much more to it than just pulling the trigger.

Learning to shoot a rifle accurately is much the same as being introduced to any other skill. In soccer, for instance, the beginner is taught the basic skills—like kicking, passing and shooting—before taking to the field and beginning actual play. Likewise, it is the same with rifle shooting. To shoot a rifle accurately, you must first learn and master the basic skills of *Shooting Position, Shot Preparation, Sight Picture Control, Trigger Control,* and Follow Through. These skills are known as the **FUNDAMENTALS OF RIFLE SHOOTING** because they must be performed every time you shoot a rifle.

Once you've learned the fundamental shooting skills, you'll be ready to move on to Part Three. There, you will learn how to apply them to various rifle shooting activities for a lifetime of fun and challenges.

The five rifle shooting fundamentals are:

1.	**Shooting Position**
2.	**Shot Preparation**
3.	**Sight Picture Control**
4.	**Trigger Control**
5.	**Follow Through**

Before you actually begin shooting, you have a major decision to make. Are you going to shoot from your right or your left shoulder? To determine which shoulder you will use, you must first determine which eye should be used for aiming. If you're like most people, you tend to use one eye more than the other. This eye is called the *dominant eye*. Just because you are right-handed does not mean your dominant eye is the right eye. Since the ability to clearly line up the sights with the target is critical to effective shooting, you should use your dominant eye for aiming. To determine which eye is dominant use this easy test:

- Extend your arms in front of you, placing your hands together and forming a small opening between them. Keeping both eyes open, look through the opening at an object in the distance.

- Then move your hands backwards until they touch your face - while continuing to look at the object. The eye you are now using to see the object is your dominant eye.

You should shoulder your rifle on the same side as your dominant eye.

SHOOTING POSITION

The shooting position is simply the posture of your body and rifle during the act of shooting. There are several positions and position variations that are used in rifle shooting. A knowledgeable rifle shooter should know five basic rifle shooting positions—benchrest, standing, prone, kneeling and sitting.

Even though the position of the body can vary greatly, the position of the rifle basically remains the same.

One might ask, "Why so many positions?" Surely one or two of those positions are better than the others. The truth is each position is best suited for certain conditions. The position you choose depends on the kind of shooting, the terrain, shooting time and target difficulty. In addition, the traditions and rules of the sport have greatly influenced the established positions and when they are used.

The importance of building rifle shooting skill on a foundation of good positions cannot be overemphasized. The position must give you a solid, steady hold on the target. A good shooting position involves the position of the body and the position of the rifle.

The position of the body is the arrangement of the head, torso, arms and legs, and their relationship to the target. Positioning the body is the first step in assuming every shooting position. Three conditions are essential for a good position. First, you must be *comfortable, relaxed*, and *balanced*. This means attaining as natural a body position as possible without straining your muscles. Second, the position must provide *maximum bone support*—to the extent possible use bones and not muscles to support the body and rifle. If you rely primarily on muscles to support the weight of the rifle, you will have a hard time relaxing and keeping the rifle steady. Third, your position must be *aligned with the target*. If the preceding conditions are met, the rifle will settle into a natural point of aim. The whole position must then be adjusted to align that natural point of aim on the target. Never muscle the rifle on target.

The *position of the rifle* involves the proper positioning of the rifle to the body. The rifle must be positioned against the shoulder so that you can look through the sights with your dominant eye comfortably and naturally. Alignment with the eye is essential to proper rifle position.

Correct hand and index finger placement on the rifle grip and trigger is a must in order to correctly hold the rifle and pull the trigger. Grasp the grip of the stock firmly with the lower three fingers, lightly resting the thumb on the top of the stock. Place the hand so that the index finger can pull the trigger straight to the rear.

The fore end should rest in the left hand. It is best not to grip or squeeze the fore end. However, with more powerful calibers it may be necessary to grip the fore end to maintain control when firing.

All position descriptions and photos in this book are for right-handed shooters unless designated otherwise. Shooters that shoot from the left shoulder (left-handed) will need to reverse position information.

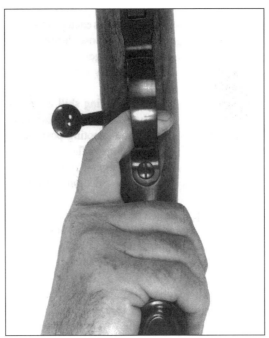

The finger placement should allow the trigger to be pulled straight to the rear.

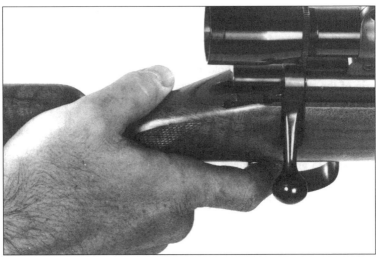

The trigger finger should be clear of the stock so it will not press on the stock while pulling the trigger.

SHOT PREPARATION

Once in position, there are two actions necessary to prepare to fire a shot. These are aiming and breath control.

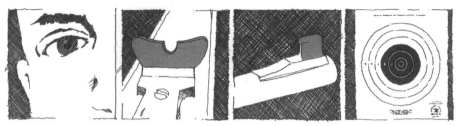

The proper alignment of the eye, sights, and target are necessary for a well-aimed shot.

Aiming, simply stated, is the process of lining up the rifle with the target. It involves the alignment of your eye, the rear sight, the front sight (or scope), and the target. Aiming is done in two steps, the first is sight alignment; the second is sight picture. The most critical step in rifle shooting is sight picture.

AIMING OPEN SIGHTS

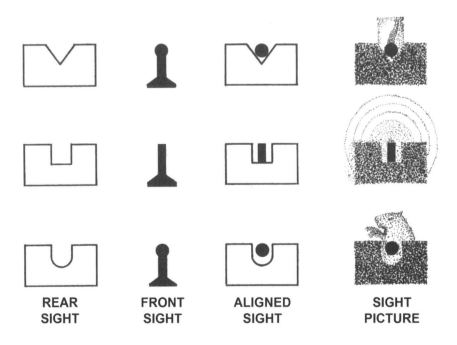

REAR SIGHT   FRONT SIGHT   ALIGNED SIGHT   SIGHT PICTURE

AIMING APERTURE SIGHTS

- **Sight alignment** is the relationship between the eye, the rear sight, and the front sight or scope. Consistent and proper sight alignment is necessary for accurate aiming. When using open sights with a post or bead front sight, you have correct sight alignment when the front sight is centered in the rear sight notch and the top of the front sight is even with the top of the rear sight. With aperture or peep sights, correct sight alignment is achieved when the front sight ring or the top of the front sight post is centered in the rear sight aperture. When using a telescopic sight, you achieve proper sight alignment by positioning your eye so that you can clearly see the entire field of view when looking through the scope.

- **Sight picture** is the relationship between the aligned sights or scope and the target. Sight picture will vary according to the type of sights you are using and the kind of target you are shooting. An aligned bead front sight should be aimed at the center of the target. The post front sight is centered on the target bullseye. The target should be centered inside an aligned front-sight ring. A scope reticle is simply centered on the target.

Breath control means stopping your breathing before you fire a shot. Breathing causes your body to move. That's fine, unless you happen to be ready to fire a shot. Continuing to breathe makes it impossible to get a steady sight picture. Before firing the shot be sure you are relaxed and comfortable. Then simply exhale normally and stop breathing. This will assist you in aiming by reducing the movement of your body and rifle in relation to the target. Generally you should hold your breath no longer than 6-8 seconds. If you are not able to fire the shot within this time, simply take a breath or two, relax and start the process over again.

SIGHT PICTURE CONTROL

Sight control is trying to keep the aligned sights or scope reticle aimed as close as possible on the center of the target. It is the most important period in the firing of a shot. Even though a proper and relaxed position has been assumed and breathing interrupted, you will still notice movement in the sight picture. This movement is natural, and only from a support, such as on a benchrest, can a shooter come close to eliminating it completely. You can, however, control and reduce the amount of movement by concentrating on achieving the proper sight picture and holding as still as possible. **You must learn to concentrate totally and consistently on sight picture control when firing.**

Controlling the movement in your sight picture is not something you can learn in one or two shooting sessions. All other fundamentals of shooting can be learned in a fairly short time, but sight picture control is practiced by champion shooters for years without achieving perfection. Absolute perfection may not be possible. However, beginning shooters will notice rapid improvement in their sight picture if they concentrate on achieving good sight picture control and practice regularly.

TRIGGER CONTROL

Once you have your best sight picture, squeeze the trigger straight back in a smooth, controlled motion until the rifle fires. This process is referred to as *trigger control*. The key is to squeeze the trigger so smoothly that it does not disturb your sight picture. Initially, you may not be able to cause the rifle to fire when the sight picture is best. But with practice, as you become familiar with your rifle's trigger, you will be able to fire the rifle when the sight picture is right.

Remember, that during this firing process you must continue to concentrate on sight picture control.

FOLLOW-THROUGH

Follow-through is the act of continuing to maintain breath control, sight picture control and trigger control immediately following the shot. Allow enough time for the rifle to return to its normal position after the recoil. This will minimize the possibility that any sudden movement during the split second between the time the shot is fired and the bullet leaves the muzzle could disturb the sight picture and radically change the bullet's path.

PART II

1. The five fundamentals of rifle shooting are:

2. Which eye is your dominant eye and from which shoulder should you shoot your rifle?

3. A rifle shooting position is made up of the position of the _____ and the _____.

4. The three conditions essential for a good shooting position are:

5. The one condition essential to proper rifle position is:

6. List the two primary elements of shot preparation.

7. The relationship between the eye and the sights in shooting a rifle is called
   _____.

8. When shooting a rifle you should concentrate on
   _____.

9. Why is it important to control the trigger?

10. What role does follow through play in firing an accurate shot?

CHAPTER 2

For those who have a choice, a .22 rimfire rifle is probably the best cartridge rifle with which to learn the fundamentals. It has no noticeable recoil and when compared to a centerfire rifle is inexpensive to shoot.

Paper targets are recommended for beginning shooters. They let you see where all your shots are striking. This is a must when learning the fundamentals of rifle shooting. Homemade targets can be easily made by drawing and coloring a circle (bullseye) on a piece of paper.

To insure initial shooting success, follow the steps outlined in this book. Then try one or more of the NRA Basic Rifle Qualification Programs found on page 121 and in the appendix of this book. They are designed to help you successfully learn the basics in the most efficient way possible using the most suitable target sizes and shooting distances.

START FROM THE BENCHREST POSITION

Now that you've determined the side on which you'll be shouldering your rifle and have been introduced to the fundamentals of rifle shooting, it's time to get started. You should start shooting from a table in a benchrest position. You'll need a sandbag or other solid support to place under the fore end of the rifle. The support helps hold your rifle steady and enables you to concentrate on learning how to shoot a good shot. If a table or bench is not available, the sandbag/support should be placed on the ground and a supported prone position used.

There are four basic steps to follow when learning any shooting position. Use them to learn the *benchrest* position.

Step 1   Study the Position—learn what a good benchrest position looks like by studying the pictures in this book.

Step 2   Practice the Position Without the Rifle—learn to put your feet, legs, body, and arms into the correct position first by getting into position behind the table without the rifle. Practice this until you are comfortable with the position.

Step 3   Practice the Position With the Rifle —add the rifle to the position you have already assumed. Again concentrate on becoming comfortable and familiar with the position.

Step 4 Align the Position with the Target—adjust the position so that the rifle points naturally at the target.

Position Characteristics of the benchrest position are:

Position of the Body

1. Body sits behind table facing target.
2. Both elbows rest on table.
3. Rifle lies in left hand which is supported by sandbag.
4. Right hand grasps rifle grip.

Position of the Rifle

Left-handed position.

5. Butt of stock is positioned against shoulder so rifle sight(s) is at eye level.

Getting into Position. Follow these steps to get into the benchrest position:

1. Take a seat at the table facing the target.
2. Grasp rifle grip with right hand and position elbows on table.
3. Lay rifle across left hand and rest hand on sandbag.
4. Position rifle against face and shoulder so that dominant eye can look through sights comfortably and naturally.

Align Position with Target

1. Vertical adjustments can be made by adjusting the height of the sand bag support.
2. Horizontal adjustments can be made by moving the sandbag support either left or right on the table or by moving the body on the chair.

DRY FIRING

The best way to start learning the shooting fundamentals is with a dry run. A technique called dry firing is used to practice the fundamentals before actually using live ammunition. Dry firing consists of closing the rifle's action on an empty (unloaded) chamber, then practicing the steps involved in firing a shot just as if the rifle were actually loaded. To do this, get into position with your rifle on the target, making sure you are comfortable and relaxed. When you feel ready, begin aiming and control your breathing. Concentrate on controlling (reducing) the movement of the sight picture and when it looks good, squeeze the trigger smoothly to the rear. After the shot "fires," follow through by continuing all of the fundamentals.

Dry fire several shots to get a feel for how much pressure is required to smoothly move the trigger without disturbing the sight picture. This requires total concentration on the sight picture at the moment of firing.

LIVE FIRING

It's now time to try the real thing with live ammunition. Shoot three to five shots at the target. Be sure to apply the same fundamentals you applied during dry firing. If you've been consistent in applying the fundamentals correctly, your shots should form a cluster or shot group on the target. At this point, don't worry about where the group is on the target. Your concern now should only be on whether the shots fall together in a group. Shoot several groups. With practice, your groups should become smaller and smaller. If your shots are scattered all over the target, then you should do more dry firing and review the fundamentals Also, be sure your sights, scope blocks or mounts are tight; any movement there can cause wild shots.

By adjusting the sights this shot group can be placed in the center of the target.

SIGHT ADJUSTMENT

Once you are shooting good groups with shots placed closely together, you are ready to adjust your sights to move your shot groups to the center of the target. This adjustment is done by moving the rear sight in the same direction you want your group to move. For example, if your group is high and left, move the rear sight down and to the right. With scopes it is necessary to move the reticle in the opposite direction of that which the shot groups should move. Most adjustment knobs are marked to show which way the knob should be turned to move a shot group in a particular direction. The instructions with most sights will tell how far one "click" or graduation of sight adjustment should move a shot at a specific distance. This can vary depending on the quality and manufacturer of the scope or sights. Be sure you understand the system before trying to adjust your sights. If your rifle does not have a click type sight adjustment, check the manufacturer's manual for means of adjustment.

Test your calculation by firing another group. The goal is to have the center of your group in the center of the target. If you're still off, continue to make adjustments until the group is in the center. Also remember that your scope or sights will likely need to be readjusted if you should shoot at a target at a different distance.

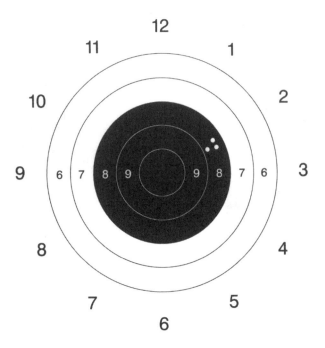

Shots on a target can be read according to the face of a clock. The shot group above is at 2 o'clock in the 8 ring.

PART II

1. Why is it best to learn the fundamentals of rifle shooting from the benchrest position?

2. List the four basic steps to follow when learning any shooting position.

3. The technique of practicing the fundamentals of shooting with an unloaded rifle is called _____.

4. What is a shot group and what can it tell you about your shooting skill?

5. Sight adjustment is accomplished by moving the rear sight in the same direction you want your _____ to move.

CHAPTER 3

RIFLE SHOOTING POSITIONS

As mentioned earlier, a number of positions may be used in rifle shooting. Once you have learned the fundamentals involved in firing a shot in the benchrest position, it's time to move on to the other basic positions: standing, prone, kneeling and sitting. Be sure to practice all safety rules and always point the muzzle in a safe direction in every shooting position. Remember the four steps you used to learn the benchrest position. These steps should be followed in learning every shooting position.

The steps to learning a position:

1. Study the position.

2. Practice the position without a rifle.

3. Practice the position with rifle.

4. Align the position with the target—How to do this is described for each of the following positions.

THE STANDING POSITION

Standing is probably the most natural and the most used position. It is the quickest and easiest position to assume. Since it provides the highest and least-stable support for the rifle, it is also the most challenging position to learn. There are two variations of the standing position—the free arm and the arm rest position. The type of shooting you are doing determines the variation you will use.

Free Arm Standing Position

The free arm position is used when the time available to fire a shot is very short or when the target is moving such as in hunting shots. Shooters who use this position should be sure they have sufficient arm strength or a rifle that is light enough to allow them to comfortably hold up the rifle.

Position Characteristics of the free arm standing position are:

Position of the Body
1. Feet are shoulder width apart.
2. Body weight is distributed equally on both feet.
3. Head and body are erect.
4. Left arm is free from body.
5. Left hand under fore end supports weight of rifle.
6. Right hand grasps rifle grip.

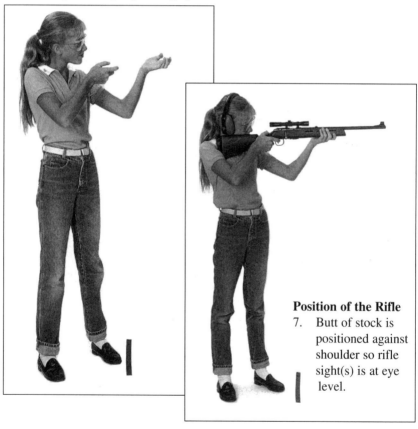

Position of the Rifle
7. Butt of stock is positioned against shoulder so rifle sight(s) is at eye level.

Getting into Position. Follow these steps to get into the free arm standing position:

1. Hold rifle in both hands, move to firing point.

2. Turn body to right of target.

3. Raise the rifle to eye level and position against shoulder.

Align Position with Target
1. Vertical adjustments can be made by simply lifting or lowering the rifle.
2. Horizontal adjustments can be made by moving the feet.

Arm Rest Standing Position

The arm rest standing position is used when a higher degree of stability and accuracy are required such as in most target events. This position is normally steadier and provides more support than the free arm variation. Shooters using a rifle that is too heavy to comfortably hold up in the free arm position should use the arm rest standing position as well.

Position Characteristics of the arm rest standing position are:

Position of the Body
1. Feet shoulder width apart.
2. Body weight is distributed equally on both feet.
3. Body bends back away from rifle.
4. Head is erect.
5. Left arm rests on side or hip.
6. Left hand supports the rifle—wrist is straight.
7. Right hand grasps the rifle grip.

Position of the Rifle
8. Butt of stock is positioned against shoulder so rifle sight(s) are at eye level.

Getting into Position. Follow these steps to get into the arm rest standing position:

1. Hold rifle in both hands, move to firing point.

2. Stand sideways to target.
3. Grasp fore end between thumb and fore-finger of left hand with wrist straight.

4. Raise rifle to eye level and position against shoulder, resting left arm against body.

Left-handed position.

Align Position with Target

1. Vertical adjustments can be made by varying the position of the left arm against the body.
2. Horizontal adjustments can be made by moving the feet.

Two time Olympic rifle gold medalist, Gary L. Anderson, demonstrates various hand positions. They allow for variation in height of the rifle, but in all cases the wrist must be kept straight for, stable support.

THE PRONE POSITION

The prone position is the steadiest of the four positions described in this chapter. Both elbows and the entire body are placed in contact with the ground, thus providing a large area of support.

Position Characteristics of the prone position are:
Position of the Body

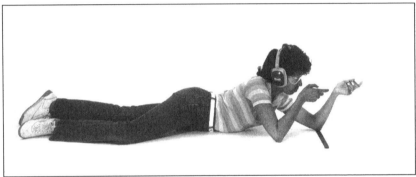

1. Body lies facing target and angled slightly to left.
2. Left elbow is extended forward of body.
3. Right knee is bent slightly.
4. Rifle fore end rests in left hand.
5. Right hand grasps rifle grip.

Position of the Rifle

6. Butt of stock is positioned against shoulder so rifle sight(s) is at eye level.

Getting into Position. Follow these steps to get into the prone position:

1. Hold rifle in both hands, move to firing point.

2. With rifle in the left hand, lower to knees.

91

3. Lower body to floor (prone position).

4. Extend the left elbow forward.

Left-handed position.

5. Raise rifle to eye level and position against shoulder.

Align Position with Target

1. Vertical adjustments can be made by moving the left hand forward (lowers rifle) or to the rear (raises rifle) on the fore end.
2. Horizontal adjustments can be made by rotating position left or right around the left elbow.

THE KNEELING POSITION

In addition to being an important target position, the kneeling position is particularly useful in the field. It is quick to assume, steadier than standing and provides the clearance necessary to shoot over terrain such as tall weeds or brush.

Position Characteristics of the kneeling position are:

Position of the Body

1. Body sits on heel of right foot.
2. Lower left leg vertical.
3. Left elbow rests on left knee.
4. Rifle fore end rests in left hand.
5. Right hand grasps rifle grip.

Position of the Rifle

6. Butt of stock is positioned against shoulder so rifle sight(s) are at eye level.

Getting into Position. Follow these steps to get into the kneeling position:

1. Hold rifle in both hands, move to firing point.

2. Turn body to right of target.

3. Drop down onto right knee and sit on right foot.

4. Adjust left leg so that lower left leg is vertical.
5. Place left elbow on left knee.

6. Raise rifle to eye level and position against shoulder.

Left-handed position.

Align Position with Target
1. Vertical adjustments can be made by moving left hand forward (lowers rifle) or to the rear (raises rifle) on the fore end.
2. Horizontal adjustments can be made by rotating the position left or right around the right foot.

In kneeling, most of your body weight should be on the right foot. You can place a tightly rolled strip of carpet, jacket, cylindrical cushion or similar support (kneeling roll) under the right foot for additional support and comfort.

THE SITTING POSITION
The sitting position is a stable position because it provides support for both elbows and that helps to steady the rifle. For hunters, sitting, like kneeling, provides more ground clearance than the prone position.

Position Characteristics of the sitting position are:
Position of the Body

1. Body sits on ground.
2. Legs are extended from body, with ankles crossed.
3. Elbows rest on legs just in front of knees.
4. Rifle fore end rests in left hand.
5. Right hand grasps rifle grip.

Position of the Rifle

6. Butt of stock is positioned against shoulder so rifle sight(s) are at eye level.

Getting into position. Follow these steps to get into the sitting position:

1. Holding rifle in both hands, move to firing point.

2. Turn body to right of target.

3. With rifle in left hand, sit down.

4. Extend legs, crossing left ankle over right.

5. Place elbows forward of knees.

6. Raise rifle to eye level and position against shoulder.

A variation of the sitting position.

Left-handed position.

Align Position with Target
1. Vertical adjustments can be made by moving the left hand forward (lower rifle) or to the rear (raises rifle) on the fore-arm.
2. Horizontal adjustments can be made by rotating the position left or right around buttocks.

USING THE RIFLE SLING

When hunting or target shooting, any type of rest supporting the rifle's fore end will greatly aid the shooter with the difficult task of holding the rifle steady. In the prone, sitting and kneeling shooting positions, a sling is recommended to *support* the rifle so the muscles of the arm won't have to. All target shooting in these positions is done with a sling to produce the highest possible stability and scores. Even during hunting, when you may have to shoot quickly, taking a few extra seconds to use a sling will return big dividends in making an accurate shot.

Hasty Sling

Hunting rifles frequently have a sling designed primarily to carry the rifle. If this carrying sling is used as a "hasty sling," it can add some support to make the position steadier. As its name implies it can be brought into position quickly. To use a sling in this manner:

1. Place upper left arm between sling and rifle.

2. Swing hand and forearm in an outward, circular motion to wrap arm around sling and place hand under rifle's fore end.

3. Bring rifle to eye level position against shoulder.

Loop Sling

A second type of sling called the "loop sling" is commonly used in target shooting and can also be used in hunting when sufficient time is available. It takes longer to put on but provides far more support than the hasty sling. Here's how to use the loop sling:

1. Open sling's loop.

2. Twist loop clockwise one-half turn.

3. Place loop high on left arm, then tighten sling keeper.

4. Wrap arm around sling using a clockwise movement so that sling comes across back of left hand and forearm.

5. Get into position with sling loosened. Tighten sling so that it—not muscles—hold rifle up in position (Once the sling is adjusted for length, it should not need to be readjusted each time the shooter gets into position.)

Regardless of your shooting plans, it's important that you master all five of the standard firing positions. The steps may seem a bit complicated and in some cases, even awkward at first. The awkwardness you experience at the beginning will help you monitor your development as a shooter. As you progress and your shooting improves, the positions will feel more natural. Your ultimate goal in getting good results from your shooting positions can be summed up in these words: **Practice = Good Shooting!**

PART II

1. Name the five basic rifle shooting positions.

2. The two variations of the standing position are:

3. The hasty sling technique is often used in the sport of _____.

4. What is the advantage of a hasty sling?

5. The _____ sling is commonly used in competitive target shooting.

6. Practice equals _____.

CHAPTER 4

USING THE SHOTGUN AS A RIFLE

Today an increasing number of people are using shotguns as rifles. They can be very effective up to 75 yards. Just as with rifles, shotgun accuracy depends on several factors. First and foremost is your marksmanship skill. The skills required to aim and shoot a shotgun are precisely the same as those required to shoot a rifle accurately. In addition, a shotgun must be equipped with adjustable sights or a scope so that it can be sighted in and aimed. You

Shotguns manufactured to be used with slugs normally come with adjustable sights.

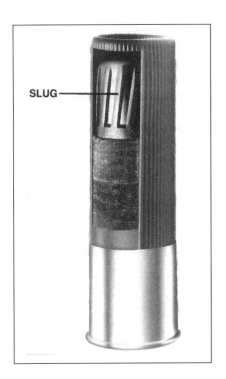

SLUG

must also know which ammunition will perform best in your shotgun barrel. Time spent on a range to find the right combination is essential. Last but not least is practice. You must become confident in your ability to shoot a shotgun accurately.

Shotguns manufactured to be used with slugs normally come with adjustable sights.

A single shotgun projectile is called a *slug*. The slug is generally a cup-shaped piece of lead approximately the diameter of the bore of the shotgun barrel. A shotgun slug with grooves and ridges on its outer surface is called a *rifled slug*. Such rifling contributes little to flight stability. The nose-heavy rifled slug gains its stability from its design that is similar to that of a badminton bird. Slugs can be fired through the barrel of any choke constriction without damaging the choke. This is because the slug is soft lead and the choke is hard steel. Any shotgun, 20 gauge or larger, is adequate for hunting, but the most often used gauge for big game is a 12 gauge. Most manufacturers today market shotguns specifically designed for slug shooting.

Nevertheless, slug-shooting shotguns are often referred to as "brush busters," implying that a slug will shoot through brush and still maintain its accuracy. However, all projectiles regardless of whether they are shot from a rifle or a shotgun are subject to deflection when they strike any foreign object, brush included. Therefore, a shooter must have a clear and unobstructed view of the target in order to fire a safe and accurate shot.

Remember, even though a shotgun slug is only accurate up to approximately 75 yards, it can still travel a distance of nearly 1,000 yards. You must apply all gun safety rules and be sure of your target and *what's beyond*.

A more recent innovation in shotgun ammunition for big game incorporates a pistol bullet design for hunting encased in a plastic cup called a *sabot*. When used with specially designed rifled barrels, shotguns firing these sabot rounds are capable of acceptable groups out to 150 yards or more.

PART II

1. Name three major factors affecting the accuracy of a slug shotgun.

2. A shotgun slug is accurate up to _____ yards, but can travel a distance of _____ yards.

THE WORLD

OF

RIFLE SHOOTING

OPPORTUNITIES

CHAPTER 1

MARKSMANSHIP—A SKILL THAT LASTS A LIFETIME

Learning how to use your rifle safely and accurately is only the beginning. As a new shooter, a whole new world of sport and recreation is open to you. It is a world of shooting activities known by millions world wide. It is a world that offers you many challenging, exciting and satisfying opportunities.

So where do you go from here? The first thing on your agenda will be to develop and improve upon the skills you've learned from this book. Regardless of your ultimate goal, the rewards of rifle shooting are directly related to your ability to perform up to your potential. What this means is *practice*. You won't become an expert rifle shot overnight; Annie Oakley and Lones Wigger were once beginners too. But if you stay with it, faithfully follow the fundamentals and never forget to have a good time, you'll be amazed at just how quickly you will progress.

Your development, not to mention enjoyment, will come even faster if you become involved in one of the many available shooting activities. The best way to learn, and to have fun in the process, is to do it with others who share your interest.

Shooting is a sport for *participants*. As you begin to develop your skills, you'll find yourself moving toward shooting activities that involve others. Quite simply, you learn more quickly in the company of like-minded people. Beyond that, your participation in shooting activities will open the door to new friendships, new interests and new ways of getting the most out of your leisure time. As you begin to channel your interests, you'll soon discover that you've acquired skills and ventured into a pastime that lasts a lifetime.

IMPROVING THROUGH TRAINING

This handbook has been designed to teach you the basics of rifle shooting. It cannot, however, provide one valuable learning component: feedback. It's much easier to acquire good habits than to break bad ones. One of the quickest and most effective ways of learning to shoot properly is to have an expert teach you. You can get that expert guidance by enrolling in an NRA Basic Rifle Shooting Course.

Throughout America, thousands of NRA Certified Instructors teach these courses each year. The NRA's Training Department can put you in touch with an instructor in your area.

Attending a course conducted by an NRA Certified Instructor in your community will get your shooting activities off to a safe and successful start.

There are many other training opportunities that will help you go beyond the basics. Training camps and clinics in rifle are offered at the beginner, intermediate and advanced level. Programs available to junior shooters include the National Instructor-Junior School for smallbore rifle. The NRA Masters Camp Program provides a similar opportunity for adults. Each of these camps provide opportunities for intensive training under the guidance of the finest instructors and coaches in the United States. In addition, NRA Gunsmithing Schools offer short-term courses (ranging from one day to two weeks in length) in rifle customizing, repair, and maintenance.

RECREATIONAL SHOOTING

The local rifle range is a good place to enjoy
shooting and make new friends.

119

The majority of shooters engage in rifle shooting simply for the fun of it. General recreational shooting or shooting for relaxation and personal fulfillment is enjoyed by millions of people throughout the U.S. The opportunity to go to a range to practice marksmanship skills enables you to enjoy the companionship, social activities, and new friends that are all a part of recreational shooting.

QUALIFICATION SHOOTING

Another exciting way to improve your shooting skills is to shoot one of the many NRA rifle qualification awards programs. These programs combine a friendly learning environment with recognition for moving up the shooting ladder. Qualification programs establish criteria for earning awards according to skill level. Challenging, but attainable, requirements are provided for beginning, intermediate ,and advanced shooters. Each time you win an award recognizing your proficiency at your current level, you'll be inspired to work toward achieving the more difficult standards of the next level. Awards are available at pro-marksman, marksman, marksman first-class, sharpshooter, expert, and distinguished expert levels. They include patches, medals, pins, and achievement certificates.

Shooting for these nationally recognized qualification awards makes practice more fun. A wide range of rifle qualification courses are offered, matching almost every type of rifle shooting activity. A booklet covering each of the qualification courses is available from the NRA Program Materials Center.

NRA RIFLE QUALIFICATION COURSES

International Air Rifle	This course is shot at 10 meters using any safe .177 caliber air rifle with any sight not containing a lens or system of lenses.
4-Position Rifle	This course is designed for BB, air, and smallbore rifles. BB guns must be smoothbore, spring-type air. Air rifles are .177 caliber skirted pellets, and any safe .22 rimfire rifle without telescopic sights or palm rests may be used.
Light Rifle	This course can be fired at 50 feet or 50 yards with a .22 caliber rimfire rifle that weighs 8 1/2 lbs or less including sights.
American Rifleman	This course can be shot with .177 air rifle or any .22 caliber rimfire rifle. Air rifle distance is 10 meters. Smallbore is shot from 50 feet (3-Position) or 50 feet to 100 yards in prone course.
Sport Shooting	This course is designed especially for your favorite hunting rifle and may be shot with any safe rifle whether it is a cartridge firing, air rifle, or muzzle-loading rifle.
High Power	This course is shot with any safe U.S. military service rifle, or centerfire rifle with metallic sights and a magazine capable of holding not less than five rounds may be used.
JROTC Rifle	Designed for Junior ROTC shooters. There is a course of fire for air rifle, sporter, and precision shot at 10 meters, as well as a smallbore rifle course shot at 50 feet.

COMPETITIVE ACTIVITIES

Rifle competition spans from local club matches to the Olympic Games. It is a great way to develop rifle shooting skills.

As a new shooter, you may not be thinking too much about competing against others in competitive tournaments. Granted, you're hardly ready for the Olympics, but that doesn't mean you can't experience the thrill and challenge of competition right now. NRA competitive shooting sports programs let you test your skills against others at your level of ability.

NRA-sanctioned competitions normally divide shooters into classes according to their ability so that shooters compete against others with national classification card that will identify your skill level. Some tournaments have a tyro or unclassified class for shooters shooting their first match.

Shooting has extensive opportunities to train and compete at all levels of competitions-local, state, regional, national, international and ultimately the Olympic Games.

Schedules of local, national, and international competitions are listed in *Shooting Sports USA*. This monthly NRA publication for competitive shooters also has many feature articles. Subscription information is available from the NRA's Competitive Shooting Division.

Rifle shooting is a college sport, sanctioned by the National Collegiate Athletic Association with an NCAA national championship held annually. Collegiate All-American shooters are honored each year by the NRA. Athletic scholarships for rifle are available from many institutions of higher learning. For further information on collegiate shooting, contact the NRA Competitive Shooting Division.

U.S. WORLD AND OLYMPIC RIFLE CHAMPIONS

The World Shooting Championships and Olympic Games shooting events offer a supreme test of a rifle shooter's skill. Shooters who compete represent the best shooters of all countries in the world. U.S. Shooting Team members have won many gold medals in the rifle events in these championships that include 300 Meter Free Rifle (centerfire), 50 Meter Free Rifle (rimfire), 50 Meter Sport Rifle (rimfire), 300 Meter Standard Rifle (centerfire), and 10 Meter Air Rifle. Shooting is done in prone, kneeling, and standing positions. The chart below honors the achievements of several U.S. World and Olympic rifle champions since 1947.

NAME	COMPETITION	YEAR
Donald Adams	World Champion	1966
Gary Anderson	World Champion	1962, 1966
	Olympic Champion	1964, 1968
Lanny Bassham	World Champion (5 events)	1974,1978
	Olympic Champion	1976
David Boyd	World Champion	1966

Arthur Cook	World Champion	1949
	Olympic Champion	1948
Glen Dubis	World Champion (2 events)	1986, 1990, 1994
Matthew Emmons	World Champion	2002
	Olympic Champion	2004
Edward Etzel	Olympic Champion	1984
John Foster	World Champion	1966, 1970, 1974
Joseph Hein	Junior World Champion	2002
Arthur Jackson	World Champion (3 events)	1949, 1952
Wanda Jewell	World Champion (2 events)	1978
Nancy Johnson	Olympic Champion	2000
David Kimes	World Champion	1974, 1978
Launi Meili	Olympic Champion	1992
Charles Metz Jr.	Junior World Champion	1994
Karen Monez	World Champion	1979
Margaret Murdock	World Champion (4 events)	1966, 1970, 1974
Jason Parker	World Champion	2002
Tommy Pool	World Champion	1962
Sue Ann Sandusky	World Champion	1978
Pat Spurgin	Olympic Champion	1984
Thomas Tamas	World Champion	1998
Lones Wigger	World Champion	1974, 1978
	Olympic Champion	1964, 1972
Verle Wright	World Champion (2 events)	1958
John Writer	World Champion	1970, 1974
	Olympic Champion	1972

HUNTING

Hunting is a pastime enjoyed by millions every year.

Hunting began as an act of survival by early man and is one of today's most popular participant sports. The challenge of the outdoors, the test of game stalking and shooting abilities, and the enjoyment of wildlife are just a few of the reasons more than 18 million hunters take to the field each year.

Learning to be a good rifle marksman is a key to successful and responsible hunting. Shots taken at game are effective only if they strike the vital area—a small area requiring precise shooting skills. Shots that miss that area are likely to wound game.

A responsible hunter knows and respects the limits of his equipment and personal marksmanship ability. Taking a shot when the hunter is not reasonably sure of hitting the game's vital area is irresponsible. If a hunter cannot consistently hit a target the size of the game's vital area beyond 100 yards in range practice, then that is the limit for responsible shots he can take in the field. The way to extend those limits is through regular practice. Marksmanship does contribute to better hunting.

Sooner or later you may have the opportunity to try hunting. If so, you should enroll in a hunter education course offered by your fish and game or wildlife agency. Through these courses, you can find out about hunting opportunities in your community and state. Most states require the course before they will issue you a hunting license.

The NRA offers many services to the hunter. They include information on seasons, regulations and legislative issues; recognition programs; the *American Hunter* magazine; the NRA Youth Hunter Education Challenge; and the NRA Hunter Clinics, providing intensified training for a variety of hunting skills. For information, write or call the NRA Hunter Services Department.

.22 RIMFIRE RIFLES

Sporter—used for general all-around, inexpensive recreational target shooting, and small game hunting. A good beginning rifle.

Standard Target—used for smallbore bullseye competitive target shooting.

Free Rifle—used for Olympic style smallbore bullseye competitive target shooting.

Running Target—used for Olympic style running target competition.

Silhouette Target—used for smallbore silhouette competitive target shooting.

127

Biathlon Target—designed for use in biathlon (ski-ing/shooting) competition.

CENTERFIRE RIFLES

Sporter—the most common centerfire rifle. Available in a wide range of calibers from .17 to .458. Used primarily for hunting and recreational target shooting. Depending on caliber, it is used to shoot at varying distances and from all shooting positions.

Varmint—Very similar to a sporter rifle, except that it has a heavier barrel. It is almost always scoped for use in shooting varmints at fairly long ranges from a supported position.

Standard Target—used for the U.S. National standard highpower bullseye competitive target shooting event.

Silhouette Target—used for highpower silhouette competitive target shooting.

Service—used for highpower bullseye competitive target shooting that is restricted to military type rifles.

Free Rifle—used for 300 meter bullseye competitive target shooting.

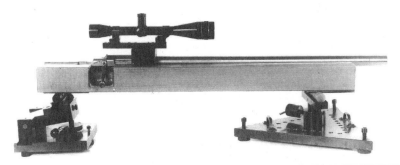

Benchrest—used for precision competitive target shooting. Shot from a benchrest using highpowered scopes.

PART III

1. How can you locate an NRA Certified Rifle Instructor in your area?

2. Name some of the shooting camps that are available to you through the NRA.

3. What are the award levels in the marksmanship qualifications program?

4. What are the advantages of having an NRA national classification card?

5. Information on NRA Hunter Clinics and other hunter programs can be obtained by contacting the _____ Department of the NRA.

CHAPTER 2

B U Y I N G   A   R I F L E

When you decide to purchase a rifle, your choice will depend on a number of variables, all of which boil down to your intended use and personal preference. Some factors influencing your choice may include the kind of shooting you intend to do, distances involved, your age and size, what friends shoot, cost and special interests. Each rifle shooting activity or sport has spawned many different types of rifles that are adapted specifically for the conditions and rules of that sport.

There are different stock styles, actions, sights, calibers and barrel lengths. Weight and special design features are also important factors to consider.

Take your time in evaluating the many models of rifles available.

Your local library or bookstore is a good place to begin your investigation of the subject. A visit to sporting goods or gun specialty stores is also a must. Find a knowledgeable salesperson to explain the features of models you're interested in, and be specific about your interests, plans for use, and budget. Manufacturers' catalogs are usually updated annually and give you a thorough rundown on various models available, their features, accessories, and prices. Take your time. Don't buy on impulse or a quick sales pitch.

Another good method of narrowing your choice is by talking with experienced shooters who know a lot about the shooting activity that interests you. If you have friends or acquaintances who are shooters, they'll enjoy sharing their experiences with you. If not, pay a visit to your local gun club or rifle range. You'll find plenty of helpful advisers.

As an NRA member, you can receive the *American Rifleman* or *American Hunter*. These magazines feature rifle articles and new product reviews. In addition, the NRA offers a full line of current shooting books you can purchase.

NRA publications provide an excellent source of information on rifles and shooting.

KNOW FIREARM LAWS

Information on firearm laws can be acquired from appropriate governmental agencies or from the NRA Research and Information Division.

Your rifle selection process should include a review of laws in your area that pertain to the purchase, ownership, use, possession and carrying of firearms. These laws vary widely according to community and state. You have both a legal obligation and a responsibility to follow them. Penalties for firearm violations can be severe.

SELECT A RIFLE THAT FITS

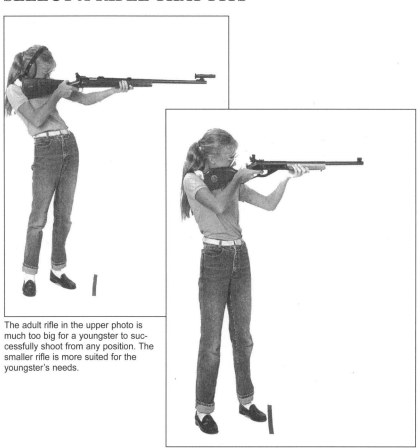

The adult rifle in the upper photo is much too big for a youngster to successfully shoot from any position. The smaller rifle is more suited for the youngster's needs.

Rifle fit centers on the stock. The majority of rifle models manufactured today have standard stock dimensions designed to fit the average-sized adult. Many manufacturers also produce youth models with smaller or adjustable dimensions suitable to a smaller or growing person's physique. In the majority of cases these rifles are more than adequate for deliberate unhurried shots. Exact stock fit becomes more important when shooting competitively, at moving targets or where quick shots or heavy recoil are involved.

There are two important fit considerations—the length and comb of the stock. For youngsters, or adults with short arms or small stature, standard-length stocks are often too long. The solution is simple: have it cut down to an appropriate size by a competent gunsmith experienced in fitting stocks. If the stock is too short, you can simply add a slip-on pad or spacer plates to lengthen it. A good starting point to check stock length is to place the butt in the crook of the arm. If the hand reaches the pistol grip and trigger comfortably, the stock length should be reasonably close to the correct length.

The comb of the stock can also affect general gun fit. A comb that is too high prevents proper alignment of the eye with the sights. It can be fixed either by raising the height of the scope or sights or by removing wood from the comb. A comb that is too low does not provide support for the face when the eye is aligned with the sights. This can be corrected by using lower sights or by taping layers of hard rubber or similar material over the comb. Commercial add-on cheek pieces are also available.

It's a good idea to spend time on the range with friends or an instructor trying different rifles. This should give you a pretty good idea of what feels comfortable.

BEFORE YOU BUY

In buying any gun, answer these questions before you make a choice. If it's a *used* gun, take additional care with your decision.

1. How do you plan to use the rifle? Is it multi-purpose or specific? What are the best caliber, weight, and sights for such use?
2. Is ammunition readily available? How much will ammunition cost for the amount of shooting you plan to do? Can it be reloaded?
3. How much do you want to spend for a rifle?
4. Have you done your homework? Have you studied manufacturers' catalogs? Have you looked at the various makes and models available, as well as their accessory and special feature options?
5. Is the rifle simple to operate and clean?
6. Does the rifle fit you or can it be easily modified to do so?
7. Have you read the warranty or guarantee?
8. Is the rifle produced by a known manufacturer? Are parts and service available and likely to be in the future? Buying quality brand names will generally insure the availability of future repairs and a return on your investment.
9. Does the rifle have a good track record for dependability?
10. Are you purchasing from a reputable dealer?
11. Can the sights be easily adjusted?

12. Can scopes, sights, and slings be easily added to accommodate changing shooting interests?
13. If you decide to trade or sell your rifle, what is its marketability? Could you get most of your money out of it?
14. Have you taken your time in making your choice? Remember, the chances are good you'll keep your rifle for life.

Your dominant eye will determine which shoulder you should shoot your rifle from. Whether a rifle is intended for right-hand or left-hand operation may be an important purchasing consideration. See page 62 of this handbook to learn how to identify your dominant eye.

ADDITIONAL POINTS IF BUYING A USED RIFLE

1. Locate the previous owner, if possible, and find out why the rifle was traded or sold.

2. A poor outward appearance on a rifle generally indicates abuse or excessive wear.

3. Make certain a reblue or refinish job has not disguised the actual past use of the rifle.

4. Check the bore for bulges or excessive wear.

5. Check the screw slots to determine if they have been abused during disassembly by an inexperienced person.

6. Check the trigger for a consistent, safe pull and smooth function.

7. Check the safety to determine if it functions properly.

8. Note that rifles in an original, unaltered condition tend to be of more value.

9. Secure advice from an expert on guns regarding a rifle's market value.

10. Check the wood for type, quality, and hairline cracks.

11. Shoot the rifle, if possible, before buying.

12. Be certain that the rifle is legally owned by the seller.

13. "You usually get what you pay for!" Beware of deals that are too good to be true—they usually are!

A YOUNGSTER'S FIRST RIFLE

Getting a first rifle is a memorable occasion, but picking the right one can be tough. Selecting a rifle that will enhance a young shooter's desire to learn to shoot is the most important consideration. The following guidelines will help:

1. Action	Any action type that may be kept open during handling and which permits easy visual access to the chamber and magazine.
2. Trigger	A two-stage trigger with a final release pressure of one to two pounds is ideal. A two-stage trigger has a take-up or movement stage and a heavier final stage where the trigger should not move perceptibly. If the trigger is the more common single-stage type, the release pressure should be two to four pounds and the trigger should have little or no movement when it is released.
3. Weight	Four and one-half to six pounds.
4. Barrel	18-22 inches in length.
5. Stock	Adjustable in length if possible—12 to 13 inches measured on a straight line from the trigger to butt. The stock grip should be sized to a youngster's hand and located to allow proper placement of the finger on the trigger. A universal stock for use by either right- or left-hand shooters is preferred. Swing swivel on fore end.
6. Sights	Any type that has a rear sight that can be readily adjusted horizontally (windage) and vertically (elevation). A scope of six power or less with internal adjustments is ideal.

SIGHT-IN YOUR RIFLE

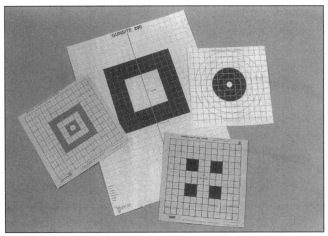

Whatever sight-in target you choose, a grid in the background is helpful in figuring sight adjustment.

Rifles that come directly from the manufacturer or have been used by other people, must be sighted-in for your eye. This is also referred to as "zeroing" the rifle. *Zero* is the sight adjustment that will allow the bullet to strike the target at the desired point of aim. To sight-in your rifle, use the following steps:

1. Be sure the chamber and bore are clean and wiped dry of any oil or grease. Also be sure all sights are attached tightly to the rifle; there must be no movement.
2. Shoot from the benchrest position at a paper target with the rifle fore end resting on sandbags or a similar stable support. Locate the support at the same position on the forearm for each shot.
3. Initially shoot at a close range (not more than 25 yards) to ensure hitting the paper. If your shots are still not on target, use a larger piece of paper until you locate them.
4. Fire groups of shots and adjust your sights according to Part Two, Chapter 2 of this handbook.
5. Once zeroed at close range, the rifle can be easily adjusted for longer distances if desired.

Remember, different ammunition, shooting distances and shooting positions can change the zero and therefore require additional sight adjustments. See "Some Tips for Success" in the appendix on page 156.

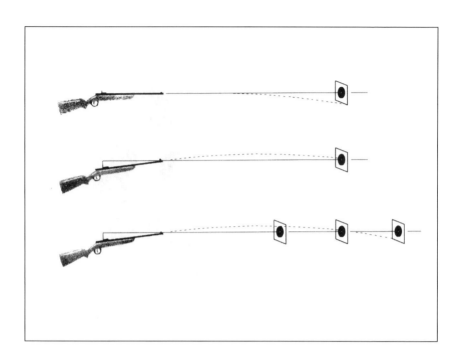

Understanding sight adjustment is essential to good marksmanship.
Top: An unzeroed rifle when shot at the target will probably miss the bullseye.
Center: Adjusting the sights places the bullet in the center of the bullseye (zero).
Bottom: A rifle zeroed for one distance will not be zeroed if fired at another distance - i.e., a 100 yard zero may hit high at 50 yards and low at 200 yards.

PART III

1. Where can you find information concerning the types of rifles available for purchase?

2. Two primary guides in determining proper stock length are _____ and _____.

3. Before buying any rifle, what are some of the things you should consider?

4. If buying a used rifle, list some things that you should check on the gun.

5. Describe the kind of rifle you would like if purchasing one (action type, caliber, sights, etc).

6. What does zeroing a rifle mean?

CHAPTER 3

SHARE THE ENJOYMENT OF SHOOTING!

Rifle shooting is one of the best family recreation activities going—and for a lifetime too!

Regardless of your age, interests and shooting ability, you'll find it hard to be alone in your favorite shooting pastime unless you choose to be. Men and women of all ages and shooting interests are organized at the local, state, and national level to participate in and promote their shooting activities. Joining shooting organizations that have these interests will enable you to meet, shoot, and work with others who share your interests. Involve your family. There are few activities that lend themselves so well to total family involvement. Take your mom and dad, son, and daughter, brothers and sisters to the range with you. You will soon see how contagious the fun of shooting can be.

JOIN A SHOOTING CLUB

Many shooters find that participation in a local shooting club is the easiest way to accomplish their shooting objectives. The local shooting club is a good place to experience the challenges of rifle shooting. NRA Certified Instructors and Coaches are usually available to help improve marksmanship skills. Many clubs have special shooting events, offer their members an opportunity to fire for qualification awards, participate in leagues, send teams to tournaments, and conduct interesting social and recreational activities.

The NRA Clubs and Associations Department can provide you with a list of NRA-enrolled or NRA-affiliated shooting clubs in your area.

YOUR STATE SHOOTING ASSOCIATION

Your NRA-affiliated state association exists to promote and support shooting activities for all state residents. Your membership and support of its work is vital to the success of the shooting programs in your state. Your state association will be happy to give you more information on its programs and services. The NRA Clubs and Associations Department can put you in touch with your state association officials.

THE NATIONAL RIFLE ASSOCIATION OF

AMERICA

The National Rifle Association of America offers a vast range of services to shooting enthusiasts, including extensive programs in such areas as safety, education, recreational shooting, training, ranges, women's issues, clubs, junior shooting, law enforcement, hunter services, legislative action, competitions, gun collecting, and gunsmithing.

The NRA is also the foremost guardian of your constitutional right to own and use firearms for all legitimate purposes.

Membership in the NRA offers many benefits. Members receive their

choices of monthly magazines packed with information for shooters, hunters and collectors. Insurance and other personal benefits are part of the membership privileges. In addition, your membership in the NRA strengthens its efforts to promote all shooting sports throughout the United States. Membership in the NRA can be a valuable part of your personal shooting experience and growth.

Whatever your shooting interest, the National Rifle Association hopes you will continue to develop and apply your skills in a safe, responsible and enjoyable manner. Joining the shooting family will give you a lifetime of fun, challenges , and personal rewards.

NOTES

PART III

1. Name several rifle shooting clubs or ranges in your area. If you are not aware of any, how can you find out about local clubs or ranges?

2. What is the purpose of a state shooting association—what is the name of yours?

3. What are some of the benefits of membership in the NRA?

APPENDIX

NRA RIFLE
SHOOTING EXERCISES

This section provides you with special exercises that help you to learn the shooting basics presented in this book. The special course described in this section can be fired using any rimfire or centerfire cartridge rifle. (It is not intended for air rifles.)

RULES

● Scores may be fired at anytime, either in formal competition or in practice.

● Any caliber cartridge rifle (rimfire or centerfire, scope or open sights) may be used. The same rifle need not be used at all times.

● Factory or reloaded ammunition may be used.

● Handmade or commercial targets may be used.

EXERCISE I:

Step 1—Learn to Shoot: Attend an NRA Basic Rifle Shooting Course or study "The Basics of Rifle Shooting" and complete the chapter reviews.

Step 2—Learn to Sight-In: Zero the rifle according to the directions on page 77 of this book.

Step 3—Learn the Fundamentals: From the benchrest position, shoot five 3 shot groups within (or touching) the bullseye as follows:

- If using a rimfire rifle—shoot at a one inch solid color bullseye (no scoring rings) at 50 feet.

- If using a centerfire rifle - shoot at a six inch solid color bullseye (no scoring rings) at 100 yards.

EXERCISE II:

Step 1—Learn the Positions: For each of the following positions, shoot two 3 shot groups within (or touching) the bullseye. (Shoot in order as listed.)

USING RIMFIRE RIFLES			USING CENTERFIRE RIFLES	
Position	Bullseye Diameter	Target Distance	Bullseye Diameter	Target Distance
Standing	3 inches	50 feet	18 inches	100 yards
Prone	2 inches	50 feet	12 inches	100 yards
Kneeling	3 inches	50 feet	18 inches	100 yards
Sitting	3 inches	50 feet	18 inches	100 yards

Step 2—Learn Sight Adjustment: Adjust the rifle sights for each of the two further distances. Fire two 3 shot groups at each distance inside the bullseye.

USING RIMFIRE RIFLES			USING CENTERFIRE RIFLES	
Position	Bullseye Diameter	Target Distance	Bullseye Diameter	Target Distance
Benchrest	3 inches	50 yards	12 inches	200 yards
	6 inches	100 yards	18 inches	300 yards

MAKE YOUR OWN TARGETS

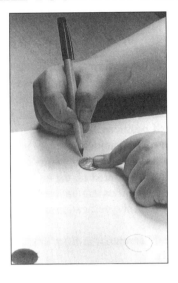

Designing or making your own targets can be as simple as using stickers or markers—and fun too!

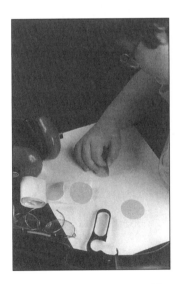

Using scrap paper, it is easy to make targets by tracing around an object and coloring in the circle. Find objects of the approximate correct size to trace around. For example, a quarter for 1 inch, a bottle or can for 3 inches, plates for 6 and 12 inches. Color in the circle with a black marker. Colors such as orange may provide better contrast with the sights.

SOME TIPS FOR SUCCESS

1. Shoot only a couple of positions in each shooting session. For a new shooter, trying to shoot all positions at once is too much to attempt and will quickly fatigue muscles.
2. Take your time—rest between each shot.
3. Even when using the same cartridge, the performance of different bullet weights or brands of ammunition can vary greatly and therefore change the bullets' point of impact on a target. To limit the likelihood of this happening, use the same ammunition and distances that you use to zero your rifle for shooting all positions.

   -Use the same brand (and type of ammunition).

   -Use the same bullet weight and type.

   -Use the same lot number (normally printed on the end of the cartridge box). This means the ammunition was produced at the same time under similar quality control specification and should perform the same when fired.
4. Use quality ammunition. "Good deal" ammunition from unknown sources may not perform consistently.
5. Wind can change a bullet's flight path and therefore the point of impact on target.

NRA MARKSMANSHIP QUALIFICATION PROGRAM

From a young shooter's first BB gun to more sophisticated air rifles, and match grade smallbore rifles, the NRA Marksmanship Qualification Program offers family fun and enjoyment that can last a lifetime.

Progression is self-paced, scores are challenging but attainable, and pins, patches, medals, and certificates are available to recognize and reward each step of marksmanship skill development.

Performance is measured against established "par" scores, and any shooter who meets or exceeds those scores is entitled to all the corresponding awards for that rating.

Eligibility: The NRA Marksmanship Qualification Program is open to everyone.

Administration: Qualification shooting can be a self-administered activity, or the activity can be administered by parents, leaders, coaches, or instructors as part of a club or group program.

Ranges: Qualification shooting can be conducted anywhere—on public ranges, at clubs, or on your own home range.

Scores: Qualifying scores can be verified by any responsible adult, such as a parent, another shooter, or a club official, coach, instructor, or range officer. Scores fired in practice sessions, leagues, or in competition may be applied toward qualification ratings.

NRA Staff: NRA staff is available to help you get started and to answer any questions that you may have. Call the NRA Qualification Program Coordinator at (703) 267-1505.

Courses of Fire: The NRA Marksmanship Qualification Program courses of fire are described in the current program booklet.

NRA SHORT-TERM GUNSMITHING SCHOOLS

NRA-affiliated gunsmithing schools offer short-term summer courses (most are approximately three to five days in length) on many interesting subjects.

There are currently four NRA-affiliated gunsmithing schools. For information, contact the schools listed below or call NRA Headquarters at (703) 267-1412.

Lassen Community College
Highway 139
P.O. Box 3000
Susanville, CA 96130
(530) 251-8800

Montgomery Community College
1011 Page Street
Troy, NC 27371
(910) 576-6222

Murray State College
One Murray Campus
Tishomingo, OK 73460
(580) 371-2371, ext. 235#

Trinidad State Junior College
600 Prospect, Campus Box 319
Trinidad, CO 81082
(719) 846-5631

NRA PUBLICATIONS & VIDEOS

The items listed below are some of the various materials available from the National Rifle Association of America. Many other items and publications are listed in the *Materials Catalog* (Item # EM09415). To inquire about any of these items or to place an order, contact the NRA Program Materials Center by telephoning (800) 336-7402 between 8:30 a.m. and 11:00 p.m. Eastern time, Monday through Friday, or Saturday and Sunday 10:00 a.m.-6:00 p.m. Please note that prices are subject to change without notice, and do not include state taxes or shipping fees.

National Rifle Association Gun Safety Rules—An illustrated multicolor, eight-panel brochure (which unfolds to feature a 16" x 17" gun rules safety poster on the reverse side) explaining the three fundamental rules of gun safety, plus rules for using and storing a gun. Item # 14080.

A Parent's Guide to Gun Safety—A brochure explaining parental responsibilities regarding gun safety for children, when and what to teach a child, and basic gun safety rules. (PK of 25) Item # 12852.

Smart & Safe: Handling Your New Gun—Designed especially for teenagers (and for adults with little or no firearm experience), this 28-page booklet provides technical, but easily understood, information regarding the safe handling of various types of pistols, rifles, and shotguns. It also addresses the responsibilities incurred by all gun users. The booklet is filled with photographs that help to explain safe gun handling. For example, readers are shown how to unload various guns and can see views of loaded and unloaded chambers. Item # 11532.

Firearm Safety and the Hunter—An illustrated, 6-panel brochure explaining safe gun handling in the field and describing field safety rules for hunters. Item # 07430.

Home Firearm Safety—A 71-page, illustrated, soft-cover book introducing and explaining the basic principles of firearm safety, with concentration on safe gun handling and storage in the home. Also explains how to identify and unload different types of firearms, discusses the various types of ammunition, and describes the proper care and cleaning of guns. Item # 14120.

The Basics of Pistol Shooting—A 127-page, illustrated, soft cover book explaining pistol parts and terms, types of ammunition, operation of various pistol actions, safety, cleaning, storage, fundamentals of pistol shooting, shooting positions, and improvement of shooting skills. Item # 13270

NRA Junior Rifle Shooting—A 134-page, illustrated, soft-cover book specifically designed for young shooters. The book not only covers such topics as gun safety, rifle parts, and shooting equipment, but also describes in detail the various rifle shooting positions. Training tips and suggestions for improving shooting skills are also discussed. Item # 09450.

The Basics of Shotgun Shooting—A 73-page illustrated, soft-cover book explaining shotgun parts and terms, types of ammunition, operation of various shotgun actions, safety, cleaning, storage, fundamentals of shotgun shooting, and improvement of shooting skills. Item # 13360.

Fundamentals of Gun Safety (VHS Format Videotape)—A 10-minute videotape, narrated by Steve Kanaly and Susan Howard of the TV series Dallas, explaining the basics of firearm safety with special emphasis on NRA's three fundamental gun safety rules. Suitable for both teenagers and adults. Item # 11560.

Eddie Eagle® GunSafe Program—A colorful, illustrated, 8-panel brochure explaining the Eddie Eagle safety program. This accident prevention program teaches young children (pre-kindergarten through third grade) what to do if they see a gun in an unsupervised situation. The program was designed through the combined efforts of such qualified professionals as teachers, school administrators, curriculum specialists, and clinical psychologists. This brochure also explains the program's fundamental safety message, and the types of teaching materials that are available. Item # 12330. Free. **Note: Initial orders of some Eddie Eagle materials are furnished free by the NRA to schools and law enforcement agencies. Youth groups and civic organizations may order the materials for a nominal charge. For more information, telephone (800) 231-0752.**

Technical Questions:
Receiving answers to technical questions is a privilege reserved for NRA members. (A non-member may submit a question if the inquiry is accompanied by a membership application.)
Each question must be in the form of a letter addressed to:

Dope Bag
NRA Publications
11250 Waples Mill Road
Fairfax, VA 22030

Each inquiry must contain the NRA member's code line from his or her membership card or from the mailing label on the *American Rifleman, American Hunter, America's 1st Freedom* or *Woman's Outlook* magazine. In addition, each letter must contain a stamped, self-addressed, legal-size envelope. Inquiries must be limited to one specific question per letter. Questions regarding the value of any type of firearm will not be accepted. Technical or historical questions will **not** be answered by telephone or by fax machine.

NRA RESOURCES

THE NRA IS HERE TO HELP-
WE'RE AS NEAR AS THE TELEPHONE OR MAILBOX!

To contact the NRA for assistance or additional information, please direct all inquiries to:

National Rifle Association of America
11250 Waples Mill Road
Fairfax, Va. 22030
Phone: (703) 267-1000
(Main Switchboard)

For questions relating to specific NRA divisions, send mail inquiries directly to the attention of those divisions at the above address, or use the following telephone numbers:

Community Service Programs Division
General information ....(703) 267-1560
Communications Department ....(703) 267-1588
Eddie Eagle® Department ....(800) 231-0752

Competitive Shooting Division
General information ....(703) 267-1450
Bianchi Cup information ....(703) 267-1478
National Matches (Camp Perry) information ....(703) 267-1451
Collegiate Shooting Department ....(703) 267-1473
Disabled Shooting Department ....(703) 267-1495
Pistol/Action Shooting Department ....(703) 267-1451
Rifle Department ....(703) 267-1475
Silhouette Department ....(703) 267-1474
Tournament Operations Department ....(703) 267-1459
Tournament Reporting Department ....(703) 267-1454
Volunteers Department ....(703) 267-1485

Education and Training Division
General information ....(703) 267-1500
Training Program information (automated voice mail)...............(703) 267-1430
Coach Programs ....(703) 267-1401
Gunsmithing ....(703) 267-1412
Hunter Services Department ....(703) 267-1524
Marksmanship Qualification Program and Courses ....(703) 267-1505
Training Department ....(703) 267-1431
NRA Shooting Education Update ....(703) 267-1428
Instructor Programs..(703) 267-1423
Women's Programs Department ....(800) 861-1166
Youth Programs Department ....(703) 267-1596

Field Operations Division
General information ....(703) 267-1340
Clubs and Associations Department ....(703) 267-1348
Friends of NRA ....(703) 267-1361
Range Development ....(703) 267-1348

General Counsel's Office ....(703) 267-1250

Institute for Legislative Action
Research and information ....(703) 267-1170

Members' Insurance
Life, Accident, & Health ....(877) 672-3006

Membership Division
All locations ....(800) NRA-3888

National Firearms Museum
Gun Collecting ....(703) 267-1600
Museum ....(703) 267-1600

Other NRA resources can be contacted at the following addresses and phone numbers:

Club Liability Insurance
    Lockton Risk Services
    Plan Administrator
    P.O. Box 410679
    Kansas City, MO 64141-0679
    For information ....(877) 487-5407

NRA Program Materials Center
    NRA Program Materials Center
    P.O. Box 5000
    Kearneysville, WV 25430-5000
    Information and credit card charges ....(800) 336-7402

To join NRA today, or for additional information regarding membership, please call (800) NRA-3888. Your membership dues can be charged to VISA, MasterCard, American Express, or Discover.

FACTS ABOUT THE NRA

Established in 1871, the National Rifle Association of America is a non-profit organization supported entirely by membership fees and by donations from public-spirited citizens.

The NRA does not receive any appropriations from Congress, nor is it a trade organization. It is not affiliated with any firearm or ammunition manufacturers or with any businesses that deal in firearms or ammunition.

Originally formed to promote marksmanship training, the NRA has since reached out to establish a wide variety of activities, ranging from gun safety programs for children and adults to gun collecting and gunsmithing. Hundreds of thousands of law enforcement personnel have received training from NRA-certified instructors in the firearm skills needed to protect themselves and the public. In addition, clubs enrolled or affiliated with the NRA exist in communities across the nation, teaching youths and adults gun safety, marksmanship, and responsibility while also providing recreational activities.

The membership roster of the NRA has included seven Presidents of the United States, two Chief Justices of the U.S. Supreme Court, and many of America's outstanding diplomats, military leaders, members of Congress, and other public officials.

The NRA cooperates with federal agencies, all branches of the U.S. Armed Forces, and state and local governments that are interested in training and safety programs.

The basic goals of the NRA are to:

- Protect and defend the Constitution of the United States, especially in regard to the Second Amendment right of the individual citizen to keep and bear arms.
- Promote public safety, law and order, and the national defense.
- Train citizens and members of law enforcement agencies and the armed forces in the safe handling and efficient use of firearms.
- Foster and promote the shooting sports at local, state, regional, national, and international levels.

• Promote hunter safety and proper wildlife management.
For additional information about the NRA, including programs, publications, and membership, contact:

National Rifle Association of America
11250 Waples Mill Road
Fairfax, Va. 22030
Phone: (703) 267-1000
(Main Switchboard)